Family of Faith Library

W9-BJD-990

MORAL EDUCATION: A HANDBOOK FOR TEACHERS

**insights and practical strategies
for helping adolescents to become more
caring, thoughtful, and responsible persons**

ROBERT T. HALL

Property of
FAMILY OF FAITH
LIBRARY

 Winston Press 430 Oak Grove, Minneapolis, Minnesota 55403

For Sylvia and Willis Hall
and Mollie and Bill Stevens

Copyright © 1979 by Winston Press, Inc.

Library of Congress Catalog Card Number: 78-59406

ISBN: 0-03-045686-X

Printed in the United States of America

All rights reserved. No part of this book may be
reproduced or used in any form without written permission
from Winston Press, Inc.

Winston Press, Inc.
430 Oak Grove
Minneapolis, MN 55403

Acknowledgments

The Moral Education Project, of which this book is a product, was begun with the support of a grant from the National Endowment for the Humanities. Without the Endowment's assistance, this volume would not have been written. I am especially grateful to our program officer, Dr. William Russell, for his helpful advice and endless patience.

The Moral Education Project is the continuation of an effort in the field of moral education on which Dr. John U. Davis of Bethany College and I have collaborated since the beginning of this decade. We gratefully acknowledge the continued support of The College of Steubenville and Bethany College.

Among the many colleagues whose advice and help have contributed to the development of these materials, I owe special thanks to John Davis, for asking all the right questions; to George Burns and Janet Rodriguez, two high school teachers whose specific contributions are noted later in this volume; and to Barry Beyer and John Geiger, who have given freely of their insights and ideas. I would also like to acknowledge with appreciation the helpful cooperation of many teachers, administrators, and students at Brooke and Wheeling High Schools in West Virginia.

Special thanks are also due to Misha Adulewicz, who typed most of the working draft of this manuscript and completed the final copy in record time.

Bethany, West Virginia
February, 1978

Contents

Part I:
Foundations

Chapter 1:
The Hard Line vs. the Soft Line: The Dilemma of Moral Education

Moral Education: Responding to a Need

Moral education is a very real concern of our age. Many of us feel as if we're losing our moral sensitivities; the shock of the Nazi era, the Cold War, and a multitude of civil conflicts have combined to destroy our confidence in the inevitability of human progress toward peace and prosperity. Watergate has undermined our faith in government, while the exposure of business payoffs in foreign countries and of windfall profits on human necessities reflects the corruption of our economic system.

On the personal level, we seem to be losing our ability to guide ourselves into happy, secure lives. Many of us are morally numb or confused. We turn to psychologists—and pseudo-psychologists—for help, and seek identity and security in radical religious movements. At the base of all this, according to one social theory, is the fact that we're no longer fulfilled in our occupations, professions, and personal relationships, and have lost our sense of what life means.

Moral education alone can't solve these social and emotional problems; it isn't a cure-all. At best, it can act as a long-range influence on the recovery of moral sensitivity if it's used to help young people make more rational decisions and become more aware of value considerations when attempting to chart the courses of their own lives.

The field of moral education is relatively new, and one way of gaining some perspective on it is to consider how it's perceived by people of widely differing points of view. These perceptions can be separated into two extremes: the <u>hard</u>

line approach, and the soft line approach. While they reflect similar concerns, each makes a unique set of demands and proposals.

The Hard Line Approach to Moral Education

In the face of recent events and social conditions, a number of people have begun to call for a return to the moral standards of our forebears and/or the Bible—or, in many cases, to what they imagine or interpret those standards to have been. What we need, they say, is to go back to the absolute, eternal principles of right and wrong, to teach them to our children, and to do a better job of upholding them ourselves. While a lot can be said for the idea of personal commitment to definite moral values which lies at the center of this position, it's educationally unsound for a number of reasons.

The Hard Line and Public Education

First, this approach is incompatible with the nature and objectives of public education in a free and pluralistic society. Based on the notion that there's one code of moral standards which is known and accepted by all to be unshakeably true, it presumes that public schools are responsible for teaching this code. One major flaw lies in the fact that no such moral or religious uniformity exists in Western society. There may have been times in our history when people held so many moral and religious beliefs in common that a sort of universal agreement seemed to be in effect; as things stand now, however, the moral consensus of society extends only to certain very basic values, and certainly not to any particular moral code. The question of what's moral and what isn't causes great controversy today, as is evident in such volatile issues as abortion, capital punishment, and the problem of deciding when a human being is legally dead. In short, the principles of our forebears and the commandments of the Bible (all of which have been interpreted in different ways by different people under different circumstances) are no longer seen as constituting a set of moral rules which can or should be taught to our children.

Public education, by definition, must be responsible to the entire community; when it promotes any single moral code or perspective—whether Catholic, Humanist, or Buddhist—it fails in its public responsibility. The public at large does seem to agree somewhat on certain basic social and personal values, and while these can provide a definite foundation for some aspects of moral education, this isn't at all the same as teaching a single, absolute code of moral behavior. The public educator's first response to the hard line, then, must be to insist that no universally accepted moral code exists. The area between right and wrong is often gray, and no educator can presume to define its limits.

The Hard Line and Social Conformity

A second fault of the hard line approach is that any effort to teach a single moral code in a pluralistic society such as ours is bound to fail. In fact, attempts like these can be seen as actually contributing to the moral crisis of our age. When people are taught only to "follow the rules" whether or not they understand the reasons behind the rules, they begin to lose their sense of self and feel as if their lives are meaningless.

The generation of people currently in their 50's or 60's defined moral responsibility as "following the rules"; as conforming to societal norms without bothering to question their validity. To many, the great moral principle of this generation was "What will the neighbors think?" while the basic issues of equality, justice for all, and responsibility for the welfare of others were seldom considered. Whatever the free market system generated—which was often inequality and injustice—was unquestioningly accepted as "natural law." This perspective fit right in with the image of society as a "melting pot," in which individual or ethnic standards and characteristics were supposed to slowly dissolve and change until everybody believed in the same things and accepted the same distinctions between right and wrong. The assumptions of the "melting pot" theory were, of course, fallacious, and the response they deserved was seen in the fact that the next generation rebelled against them when they reached college age in the 1960's.

In a pluralistic society—or in a society like ours, which has only recently recognized its own pluralistic nature—moral positions are constantly being challenged by contrary beliefs and opinions. Moral rules make little sense, especially to young people, unless they're founded on good reasons which can be clearly explained. "What will the neighbors think?" and "Because I said so" don't count for much when one is searching for his or her own way to a good life in a confused and confusing world. Rather than advocating strict rules and codes of behavior, then, we need to help young people think through the problems they face. We need to guide them in considering the alternatives (both old and new), in deciding for themselves what actions, values, and lifestyles they're going to adopt, and in recognizing the social responsibilities of their decisions.

This doesn't mean that we should simply tell young people to follow their own feelings. If we can help them to think rationally about the decisions they'll be making during their lives, and to consider the basic values and lifestyles that have been passed on to us through history, we'll be giving them something important: the tools or skills they can use to develop their own moral perspectives. In short, the rules in and of themselves are no longer sufficient; we must help young people to recover the value commitments which lie behind the rules. We must aid them in rethinking and reliving the experiences which gave rise to those rules. In a world in which people are constantly being challenged to defend their commitments and lifestyles, it's not enough to be taught an "approved" moral code; we must also have some sense of its origins and worth.

Thus, these first two arguments against the hard line approach are based on the fact that we live in a morally pluralistic society. Only recently have we become aware of the fact that the "melting pot" image of conformity no longer applies; what's occurring now is that we're in the process of adopting what Mark Twain called the "tossed salad" image to replace it.

R.M. Hare, Professor of Moral Philosophy at Oxford University, addressed this fact and its implications for moral education when he said,

> There may be, even now, parts of the world in which [hard line] methods...are possible. I should guess that

these include still, certain socially isolated parts of the U.S.; Russia; China; and a few primitive tribes in out-of-the-way places where the young still have access to only one set of values, those of their elders. In such places somebody (and who it is differs in my different examples) is in a position to dictate the set of values that are to be inculcated in the young, and the inculcation is on the whole fairly successful.

But actually we have opted for a wholly different, pluralistic, liberal society; and it would be impossible, short of some kind of totalitarian revolution of the right or left, to alter this. You would have to ban, not just Lady Chatterley, but all the works of D.H. Lawrence and most of the other writers that the young read. In practice it is not possible to insulate them from the voices, some wise and some quite crazy, according to one's point of view, which compete for their attention. I do not, therefore, feel called upon to answer the question of whether it would be a good thing to put the clock back; we cannot. For as long ahead as it is possible to foresee, there will be no chance, even if it were a good thing, of seeing to it that only one set of values is available to the children in our society. We have got to try to fit them to make, for themselves, the choices with which they will inevitably be faced. And these will be choices, not just of hair styles, but of some of the most fundamental elements in their ways of life. The choices may be made explicitly and with understanding of what is happening, or they may be made by going with the crowd, which nowadays means the crowd of their own age-group; but they will be made.*

Indoctrination: The True Colors of the Hard Line

The third reason why the hard line approach to moral education is undesirable is that it isn't a form of education at all, but rather a means of indoctrination. Education becomes indoctrination whenever ideas are represented as absolutely

*R.M. Hare, "Value Education in a Pluralistic Society." Proceedings of the Philosophy of Education Society of Great Britain, January 1976.

true or right when in fact there's considerable disagreement about them. And indoctrination is wrong because it prevents people from making their own free and informed choices.

The dangers of indoctrination are especially real in the area of moral education. What's at stake here is the ultimate direction of a person's life, which is largely a matter of the values he or she develops in and through the choices he or she makes. If freedom has any meaning at all, then it certainly must include the right to choose one's own lifestyle and value orientation. Since our society holds people morally and legally responsible for their decisions and actions, we must defend their freedom of choice by giving them full and unbiased information. Since indoctrination literally takes away freedom of choice, as Robert Litke has pointed out, it's nothing short of an assault upon the person because it deprives him or her of a basic human right.*

Educators have a unique responsibility in this regard. Their calling is to teach people how to think for themselves, to respect the opinions of others, and to look for the reasons behind the traditional rules and standards—not merely to recite or memorize or accept. Only by presenting all sides of a question, and by making sure that different moral perspectives are given fair consideration, can the educator accomplish these goals. Sometimes, he or she may have to act in accordance with this obligation even when social pressures or parental desires demand otherwise.

Conflicts can be avoided, however, if the educator has a genuine appreciation of the good reasons that lie behind the different moral perspectives of various people in the community and is able to present them objectively and clearly. Moral education can and should be supportive of the guidance young people receive at home (assuming that such guidance exists, and that it's both wise and sufficient), and it will be supportive if parents and educators alike are willing and able to speak with young people in terms of reasons rather than rules alone. Parents and educators also have a choice to make, and they must be open to the idea of giving young people something more than the social conformity ethic.

*Robert Litke, "What's Wrong with Closing Minds?" in John Meyer, Brian Burhna, and John Cholvat, eds., Values Education. Waterloo, Ontario, Canada: Wilfred Laurier University Press, 1975.

The Soft Line Approach to Moral Education

At the opposite end of the spectrum of opinion on moral education are a number of people who feel that the answer to the moral crisis can be found in increased self-awareness, more fulfilling human interactions, and freedom for creative expression. We need to be more in touch with our physical and emotional selves, they say, before we can understand what we want out of life. According to this view, the moral crisis is really an identity crisis; since people don't even know who they are, they can't be expected to develop their own values, principles, or lifestyles. Proponents of this view maintain that moral education, therefore, ought to center on personal growth and interpersonal relationships and emphasize individual freedom rather than structure or authority.

The Soft Line: An Unwillingness to Take a Stand

While this very personal soft line approach—like the hard line—emphasizes some important concepts, it, too, is inadequate for public moral education. In the first place, education which attempts to be value-free, or which tries not to influence students' values, seems as incapable of encouraging young people to develop value perspectives as the older methods of indoctrination are. As Milton Rokeach, a major researcher in values, has said,

> A value education program will turn out to be illusory or self-deceptive if the sole focus is on the students' own values. Such a focus is likely to be too egocentric to be educationally effective. Self-awareness is but the opposite side of the coin of social awareness. A more genuine self-awareness will, I believe, be achieved as a result of stimulating a comparison process, in which what we find out about ourselves is compared with what we find out about significant others.*

Advocates of the soft line approach may insist that their approach hasn't been given a fair chance; enough attempts

*Milton Rokeach, "Toward a Philosophy of Value Education," in John Meyer, et al., op. cit., p. 215.

have been made to implement it to reveal many of its shortcomings, however. The doctrine of value-neutrality in education (in which teachers either avoid controversial issues or refuse to take a stand one way or another) has dominated public classrooms for a number of years and seems actually to have contributed to the moral crisis by fostering the notion that it's not important to commit oneself to any definite values at all. Value-neutrality in education has not resulted in sufficient emphasis on personal growth and development; the freedom to learn, as Carl Rogers calls it, is still noticeably absent from our classrooms. In addition, this approach hasn't always led students to develop strong personal moral standards. The fact remains that while the older methods of direct indoctrination have been counterproductive in our pluralistic society, the attempts at moral laissez-faire haven't done any better.

The Soft Line and the "Social Vacuum" Concept

A second flaw in the soft line approach is its apparent presumption that people develop values in a social vacuum—i.e., in the absence of influence, guidance, help, or direction from others. Rokeach's criticism of this approach is based on the notion that social and individual values are transmitted rather than self-generated. In other words, value-neutrality may actually decrease the student's desire for moral sensitivity and commitment. There are many indications that this is precisely what's happening, both by choice, due to the fear of indoctrination, and by default, due to the fact that teachers have been reluctant to deal with controversial value issues and seem unaware of the value questions which are raised in their classrooms every day.

The atmosphere which actually seems to be the most conducive to moral development is one in which definite value perspectives are presented in such a way as to encourage respect for differences of opinion and belief. Even if young people reject the value priorities of their elders—as many now seem to, for example, in emphasizing cooperation rather than competition, and conservation rather than exploitation of natural resources—they seem to mature more securely when they're confronted by definite moral perspectives. (Definite, by the way, isn't the same as dogmatic or absolutist.) Many psychologists and educators are now telling us that young people want their elders to take a firmer stand on moral issues, even when they themselves don't agree with the particular stand taken.

The Soft Line and the Absence of Learning

A final reason for rejecting the do-it-yourself attitude of the soft line is that there are some things in the domain of moral decision-making which can be learned. These include certain skills of moral thinking and the concepts of individual and social values which are a part of our Western cultural tradition. The fact is that people do make decisions and discuss moral problems, and there are a number of values widely held in our society which constitute a body of substantive knowledge that's an important resource for wise decision-making. A significant but subtle difference exists, however, between teaching values and teaching about values. We can, one would hope, teach young people the meaning and use of value concepts and help them to understand the place of values in our society without pressuring them to conform to any particular code.

When the intellectual skills of rational decision-making and the content of our cultural tradition are replaced by an emphasis on personal growth and adjustment, the impression is given that values are relative to and dependent on feelings alone. This contributes to the moral crisis by leaving people to fend for themselves. If we're going to take moral education seriously, we must try to recover these skills and this sense of tradition. We don't expect young people to re-invent any other subject solely by drawing from their own experience, and there's no reason why we should expect them to fabricate their own system of values without any help at all. If the hard line approach is characteristic of the middle-aged generation's emphasis on conformity for conformity's sake, then the soft line is a product of the very personal and intense search for values which has characterized the succeeding generation. We've moved from social conformity to moral individualism— from "What will the neighbors think? to "Do your own thing"—and neither extreme has proven either healthy or wise.

The Middle Way: A Creative Tension

The hard line and the soft line represent two extreme approaches to moral education. Both are unacceptable; the hard line because it's really a form of indoctrination, and the soft line because it leads to moral relativism. The problem and the challenge of moral education in our age is to find a middle way, an approach which neither forces young people to accept one set of moral rules nor gives them the impression that decision-making is all a matter of personal opinion or whim.

No one has yet charted this middle way perfectly, nor has anyone been able to provide teachers with easy solutions to the many problems which the task of moral education poses. It seems, however, that a clear understanding of the situation in terms of its extremes can provide us with some very practical guidelines. While we need to specify our objectives as carefully as we can, we must also keep in mind the limits within which we must work—i.e., the pitfalls of indoctrination on the one hand, and the insecurity of relativism on the other. If we know what we should try to avoid in moral education, we'll have a much better idea of what we should try to accomplish.

The middle way for moral education can best be seen as a creative tension between the good points of both the hard and soft lines. While each extreme taken alone has its faults and perils, each also has merits we can recognize and use.

Tradition: The Merit of the Hard Line Approach

If we separate the hard line approach into its various components, we can see that its one distinctive merit lies in its emphasis on transmitting the moral values and principles which have been passed down to us through our cultural history. The moral traditions of our society have been severely devalued and neglected in recent decades, and many young people don't seem to realize that human beings can and do make decisions for moral reasons, or that they do or don't do certain things as a matter of principle. We can use our traditions to help young people to understand and appreciate that people do hold moral values which guide their decisions and govern their lifestyles.

Our cultural heritage contains a number of compatible, incompatible, and semicompatible moral orientations. We need to expose our young people both to this diversity and to the degree of moral consensus that exists within our society. There is a tradition which can be passed on, but it isn't a single code of behavior, nor does it give all the "right" answers to moral questions. Instead, it can be seen as a sort of agreement on major values but with much room for divergent opinions and for thinking and rethinking their moral implications. What we need, then, is to approach moral education by avoiding indoctrination—by performing a kind of mental sidestepping, as it were—while at the same time handing down a sense of the meaning and significance of our society's more commonly held moral values.

Moral educators have been a little timid about this so far, perhaps out of a fear of indoctrinating their students (which is a perfectly valid fear). It's reasonable, however, to aim at teaching young people what value concepts are, what they've been in the past, and how they can act as tools in the decision-making process. Tradition is an important element of moral education, and we shouldn't discard it simply because it's often confused with indoctrination.

Freedom of Choice:
The Merit of the Soft Line Approach

The one merit of the soft line is its recognition that moral development must lead to the capability for autonomous and independent decision-making. After all, each of us is responsible for his or her own moral decisions, and we can't escape that responsibility by claiming that we're merely "going by the rules" or "following orders." Thus, we must be willing and able to encourage young people to grow and develop their own natural capabilities and moral sensitivities to a point where they're clearly able to make their own most responsible decisions. This goes hand in hand with the need to instill in young people a sense of respect for the integrity of others as responsible decision-makers; this isn't the same as saying that any opinion or decision is just as good as any other, though, or that it doesn't make any difference what one decides or how.

The teaching of the values of our cultural tradition can be quite naturally balanced by an emphasis on individual awareness and freedom of choice.

We can see where the middle way leads. Young people have a right to know about the diversity of moral perspectives, the different lifestyles that follow from them, and the degree of moral consensus that exists in our society. They also need to be encouraged to do their own decision-making and growing up. By combining the emphasis on tradition characteristic of the hard line approach with the emphasis on freedom inherent to the soft line, we should be able to come up with a workable recipe for moral education.

Defining the middle way is one thing; finding it is another. While the materials in this Handbook have been compiled in an attempt to avoid the pitfalls of indoctrination and relativism—in other words, to approach the middle way— it must be admitted that we all need to learn a great deal more about moral education and gain a great deal more practical experience before we'll be able to claim that we're totally successful.

Teaching Strategies and Objectives for a Moral Education Program: Approaching the Middle Way

Moral education as conceived in this Handbook differs from the teaching of other subjects, particularly those in which content retention is the primary objective. Because of the very practical nature of moral education, the classroom strategies contained in this text are much closer to experiential techniques than to the traditional forms of "instruction." The skills of decision-making can be built only if students practice them; empathy and awareness are developed only when one reflects on—and participates in—real-life situations; facility in interpersonal relations comes only with direct experience; and even the most basic concepts "taught" in moral education are much too broad to be reduced to definitions which could be committed to memory.

Basically, moral education requires teaching strategies which are genuinely student-centered. The "classroom materials" ultimately consist of the decisions which the students themselves make. The options and beliefs which accompany these decisions must, of course, be considered and discussed, but the moral education process is most successful when it begins and ends with choices about actions. Helping students to make better decisions (better in the sense of more informed, more rational, and more morally sensitive) requires the use of teaching strategies which focus on the actual decisions that people make. Moral education is a "therapeutic" or even "remedial" technique, then, in that it aims at improving students' performance of tasks which they already do, however well or poorly, rather than giving them completely new skills or information. All of us are used to making decisions; the goal of moral education is simply to help us get better at it.

Recognizing the need for this student-centered orientation can help the moral education teacher to gain a clearer concept of his or her task. Anyone who assumes that "teaching" moral education means the same as "giving" students something they don't have—i.e., "giving" them some "morals"—will have a hard time understanding the ideas and goals of moral education implicit in these teaching strategies. What social critic Paulo Friere calls the "banking" concept of education—in which the teacher gives something to the students and expects them to tuck it away until it's needed again—simply has no meaning here.* Instead, students should be guided in developing and improving the decision-making skills they already have. Thus, no one can say just what's being "given" and what's being "received" in the moral education process.

Once a teacher is willing to give up this "banking" concept and adopt a student-centered one instead, the task becomes much easier. Moral education is the business of helping students learn to make better decisions and, in particular, to make decisions which reflect knowledge and consideration of the importance of moral values. It isn't necessary to defend the "content" of moral education in the sense of being able to point to texts and lectures; as a process, moral education is better conceived in terms of the teaching

*Paulo Friere, Pedagogy of the Oppressed. New York: The Seabury Press, 1974.

models common to the creative arts, writing, or physical education. Teachers of these subjects aren't expected to defend their "content"; it's presumed that their work centers on improving students' skills.

The teaching strategies suggested in this Handbook are based on this student-centered orientation. They consist of activities which put students in situations designed to illustrate the various aspects of moral decisions. These activities help students to develop their decision-making skills, build value concepts useful in decision-making, and expand their competence in social interaction. The role of the teacher in these activities is best seen as that of a facilitator who plans the learning activities, designs and adapts them to the needs of a particular class, initiates and guides the interactions, and evaluates progress.

Part II of this text describes the five basic classroom strategies for using the materials contained in Part III. These strategies are presented as teaching models which can be used with materials from almost any field of interest or academic subject. In addition, they can be adapted for use with junior high and high school students and adult groups alike; their simplicity gives them flexibility. They may also be incorporated into teacher education courses, graduate education workshops, small church-group classes, and large public school classes. In other words, they can be used wherever the teacher feels they're needed—as they were during their development.

A brief description of each of the teaching strategies may prove helpful before we begin to consider them in detail.
• The Awareness Strategy includes procedures for building one's consciousness of oneself and others as decision-makers, and stresses awareness (clarification) of one's own value priorities and of the opinions of others.
• The Debate Strategy is a case-study method for gaining experience in taking positions and defending decisions.
• The Rational Strategy is a case-study method for building intellectual skills for moral reasoning.
• The Concept Strategy is an inquiry method for developing concepts of personal and social value.
• The Game Strategy consists of interaction games and role plays aimed at expanding proficiency in social relations requiring moral decisions.

Although the five strategies will be presented here as focusing on the above objectives, it will be obvious that all of them are in one way or another related to each of the more general objectives of moral education. In practice, the teacher will find that the strategies can either be used together in many ways, as presented in the classroom materials in Part III, or that they can be used separately with other teaching materials as supplementary exercises. Teachers who become skilled in using these strategies will find that they can easily create their own materials to meet the needs and interests of their particular groups.

Part II:
Five Teaching Strategies

Chapter 2:
The Awareness Strategy: Learning About Ourselves and the People Around Us

The first teaching strategy for moral education isn't, in fact, a single teaching model, but rather a collection of learning activities with a common double focus: heightening the student's awareness of his or her own feelings, values, and priorities, and encouraging empathetic understanding of the opinions and values held by others.

Values Clarification: A Source of Awareness Activities

Perhaps the best-known collection of awareness activities originated with the values clarification movement, especially from the value theory of Louis Raths, and was developed by Sidney Simon, Howard Kirschenbaum, and others.* One popular activity, for example, helps students to develop an awareness of personal decisions and preferences by asking them to list the twenty things they most like to do.** These might include simple activities, such as walking in the woods or on the beach, or expensive and time-consuming ones, like a vacation in Trinidad. When the lists are completed, the teacher asks the students to place certain letters or symbols next to the things they do alone; those which cost more than five dollars;

*The first major account of this approach is found in Louis E. Raths, Merrill Harmin, and Sidney B. Simon, Values and Teaching. Columbus, Ohio: Charles E. Merrill, 1966. A convenient collection of teaching materials is Sidney B. Simon, Leland W. Howe, and Howard Kirschenbaum, Values Clarification: A Handbook of Practical Strategies for Teachers and Students. New York: Hart Publishing Co., 1972. A good collection of essays with a helpful bibliography is Howard Kirschenbaum and Sidney B. Simon, eds., Readings in Values Clarification. Minneapolis, Minn.: Winston Press, 1973.

**Values Clarification, p. 30.

those which require particular skills; and/or those which they haven't done during the last six months. By reflecting on the list—for example, by writing essays describing themselves according to what they've learned from their lists—students gain an awareness of and insight into their own preferences and activities. A student may discover that almost everything he or she likes to do is expensive; that he or she doesn't like doing much alone; that he or she isn't willing to give time to activities which require learning new skills; or (as often is the case with adults) that during the last six months he or she has managed to do only a few of the things he or she really enjoys. Good awareness activities are those which create what some learning theorists call a cognitive disequilibrium— an awareness of the distance between what is and what might be—which in itself provides a motive for closing this gap.

Other values clarification activities, like those of Milton Rokeach, ask students to rank activities, decisions, or values in order of preference. Ranking may also be combined with analysis of the values or value priorities involved in the preferences.

Example: Which would you rather be? (Number your preferences from 1 to 6, placing the number 1 next to your first choice, the number 2 next to your second choice, and so on.)

_____ an Olympic gold-medal winner
_____ an international diplomat for the United Nations
_____ the inventor of the rotary combustion engine
_____ a rock music composer
_____ a corporation president
_____ a priest, rabbi, or minister

Why would you want to be your number 1 choice?_____
_____
What's important about the occupation you chose? _____
_____
What might be important about the others? _____
_____

Example: If you were building a new town, which would be most important to build first? Second? Third? (Place the number 1 next to your first choice, the number 2 next to your second choice, and so on.)

_____ hospital
_____ police station
_____ church
_____ sewage system
_____ grocery store
_____ school

Why is your first choice most important? _____
_____

What's important about your second choice? _____
_____

What's important about your third choice? _____
_____

These activities do two things. First, they ask students to make some choices; second, they attempt to direct their attention to some of the values behind their preferences. The questions "What's important about this choice?" and "Why is it important?" are used in place of the term "value" in these elementary exercises because many students initially don't understand what a "value" really is, even though they may use the term frequently. It can be a mistake to begin talking about moral values too quickly. Students often look for the key terms or concepts in which a teacher seems interested and can learn and use the jargon of moral discussion without ever letting the discussion affect their own daily experiences and decisions.

Awareness activities can begin simply, as the ones shown above do, and move from there to become quite complex or personal.

Example: Which of the following is most important? Which comes second? Which third, and so on?

_____ freedom of speech
_____ freedom to vote
_____ religious freedom
_____ national security
_____ economic security

Example: The inscription on Thomas Jefferson's grave says that he was author of the Declaration of Independence and the Virginia Bill of Rights and that he founded the University of Virginia. It doesn't say that he was President of the United States. Jefferson himself asked that it be written in that way.

Why do you think he requested this? _____

_____

What would you like your epitaph to say? _____

_____

These are all typical values clarification activities. The scope of the Awareness Strategy is, however, narrower in some respects and wider in others than that which is normally considered to be the values clarification approach. It's narrower in that it includes only three of Louis Rath's original seven value skills, leaving the others to be the primary focuses of other strategies. The three skills that do deal with awareness are described by Merrill Harmin and Sidney Simon as (a) "making choices on one's own, without depending on others"; (b) "being aware of one's own preferences and valuations"; and (c) "being willing to affirm one's own choices and preferences publicly."*

Empathy: Beyond Valuing

An important aspect of awareness which goes beyond valuing as such is empathy—the realization and appreciation of other people's feelings, motives, and values. Developing empathy is, of course, an objective of humanistic and social science education in general; moral education gives special attention to it.

Activities for building awareness of others can be very similar to the clarification or self-awareness exercises above. In fact, most clarification strategies can be adapted to address empathy by any one of the following methods:

• Comparison: With any of the above examples, the teacher asks students to compare their answers with those of their classmates and to write a paragraph describing what another student considers important.

• Interviews: Students are asked to interview one another for the above exercises rather than simply writing down their own

*Readings in Values Clarification, p. 13.

answers. If students are instructed to cross-examine the people they're interviewing <u>before</u> writing down the interviewees' answers, the exercise becomes a self-awareness activity for the interviewee as well as an experience in empathy for the interviewer.

- <u>Agreement and Disagreement:</u> This method can best be illustrated by an example.

Example: Choose one from each group.
(a) Would you rather
___ walk in the woods?
___ walk on the shore?
___ climb a mountain?
___ ride a bicycle?
(b) Would you rather be
___ famous?
___ wealthy?
___ happy?
(c) Which is more important to you?
___ friendship
___ security
___ self-respect
(d) What kind of person do you like most—someone who's
___ honest?
___ cheerful?
___ imaginative?
Now find someone in the class who has marked some of the same choices as you have. Then consider the <u>other</u> preferences about which you and that person <u>disagree</u>. Write a paragraph together describing your similarities and differences.

- <u>Cooperation:</u> Another technique for building awareness of others involves asking students to work in small groups to construct joint lists of choices or priorities. This method can be quite effective, especially after students have started determining their individual preferences, because the joint project often becomes a task of negotiating differences which are already acknowledged. It's even more effective in a game situation where the negotiation directly affects each player. The example above which asks students to decide what to build first in a new town works well for a cooperative project like this.

Joint decision-making to build awareness can also be used as part of the Rational Strategy (see pages 43-50) because in this approach a number of alternatives and their consequences are brought out.

• Prediction: Awareness of other people's feelings is also developed through exercises or games in which students attempt to predict one another's opinions or guess their next moves.

Example: Your task is to predict your partner's opinions on the following questions. For each one, you may ask your partner any question you wish except the question as it's written here.

(a) Would you vote for John-Boy Walton for President?

_____ Yes

_____ No

(b) Should someone in a waiting room ask another person to stop smoking if it bothers him or her?

_____ Yes

_____ No

(c) Is the man naturally the dominant partner in a marriage?

_____ Yes

_____ No

After you've attempted to predict your partner's opinions, ask him or her the questions as they're written here.

Were your predictions of his or her opinions correct? _____

_____

Could you have asked better leading questions? _____

_____

Why or why not? _____

_____

What do you think led you to make right predictions? _____

_____

What misled you to make wrong predictions? _____

_____

The activities shown here are meant to serve only as examples of clarification and awareness techniques. While they can, of course, be used on their own, they work best if they're used in conjunction with other moral education materials.

Experience shows that teachers who are familiar with these general types are usually able to create their own activities to suit their students' needs and interests and to correspond to the units they're teaching.

Discussion Skills: Another Dimension of Awareness

Since classroom discussion is such an important part of moral education, the moral education teacher should plan to devote special attention to it. Many teachers mistakenly assume that good class discussions just "happen" or that a few appropriate leading questions are all that's needed to prompt an active interchange.

Students often don't join in classroom discussions simply because they're afraid to speak out. This is especially true when their personal opinions are involved, since by voicing them they can risk teacher or peer disapproval. For awareness activities to be successful, an atmosphere conducive to the discussion of preferences and decisions needs to be created in the classroom. This lessens the risk of speaking one's mind and provides students with a sense of security.*

Students are often inhibited during class discussions because they lack skills in interpersonal relations and communications. To help them compensate for this, awareness activities may be expanded to include communication skills. This doesn't really involve much of an extension of the concept, since the ability to express oneself goes pretty much hand in hand with one's awareness of his or her own opinions. People become aware of their own feelings and beliefs when they're called upon to express them to others. The same is true for awareness of others; effective group discussions require participants to have listening as well as speaking abilities. Paying attention to others, thinking about what they have to say, and responding to them are additional ways of building empathy.

*For further discussion of this idea, the reader may want to look at Chapter 7 of Moral Education in Theory and Practice by Robert T. Hall and John U. Davis. Buffalo, N.Y.: Prometheus Books, 1975.

There are specific activities available for building discussion skills.* These can be used in the midst of discussions as well as on their own. When students don't seem to be listening to one another, for example, it helps to ask each person who wants to speak to first summarize what the person before him or her had to say. A variation of this approach includes asking students to question the previous person before going on, or instructing them to end their own statements with a question which anyone who wants to introduce a new thought must first answer.

The concept of "wait time" is also helpful. Students aren't always prepared to respond as quickly as teachers might expect them to. Techniques for taking the pressure off—even a simple statement by the teacher to the effect that students should think about a question for a moment, or write down their comments before the discussion starts—can be very useful. "Wait time" denotes the teacher's awareness that students might need a few moments for reflection, and maybe even a little help, before they're put under any pressure to respond.

Awareness and the Pressure to Conform

One value skill mentioned by Raths and Simon which deserves special attention is the public affirmation of one's values. As young people become more aware of their own values and those of others, they naturally become more aware of the differences between themselves and others. A special effort should be made in moral education to help students come to expect and appreciate these differences; this will alleviate their own fears of being different when it comes time for them to make decisions. Peer pressure is often the greatest barrier to effective and mature decision-making for young people. They act the way their friends act, or they choose the alternatives they know will be approved by their peers because they're afraid of being labeled as "different" or "strange." These fears are real because the threat is real; it's far too easy for young people to

*A helpful little book on facilitating discussion is B. Stanford and G. Stanford, Learning Discussion Skills Through Games. New York: Citation Press, 1969.

get ostracized from their social groups, and they take real risks when they do have enough courage to disagree with those groups.

The pressure to conform is one element of the moral crisis of our age which moral education can attack directly. A classroom atmosphere can be created in which students feel emotionally free to express their opinions, defend their decisions, and change their minds. The teacher can facilitate the development of this kind of atmosphere by showing interest in and concern and respect for differences of opinion. The pressure to conform can also serve as a topic for class discussion.

The examples which follow go beyond "awareness" as such, but in ways in which it's natural for these strategies to flow into one another.

Example: What would happen if you refused to let a friend cheat from your paper during a test? _____
_____

Would you lose your friend's respect? _____
_____

What's the real meaning of respect? _____
_____

How could you stop your friend from cheating and still keep him or her as a friend? _____
_____

Example: What if you got to know someone (a new person in school, for example, or a new neighbor) and your best friends didn't like him or her? _____
_____

What if you grew to like this person and felt that he or she wanted to be more of a friend, but your other friends still wouldn't accept him or her? _____
_____

What could you do? _____
_____

Would you accept the consequences? _____
_____

Role Play: What could you say to your new friend (suppose it's someone who lives next door to you) to help him or her understand that you want to be friendly but your other (closer) friends won't accept him or her?

A stronger form of this type of awareness activity—which should be used only with students who are prepared for it—is to role play a situation where one person is "put on the spot." For example, some students can be assigned to "object," "criticize," or "attack" another student's position, depending on how strong one wants the game to be, while that person has to defend himself or herself. It should be made very clear, however, that being "on the spot" is entirely a role play of limited duration. The teacher can, of course, volunteer to be "on the spot" himself or herself to demonstrate the activity. Students should also discuss the difference between criticizing a person's opinion and criticizing the person—an important distinction, and one that's crucial to moral growth.

Chapter 3:
The Debate Strategy:
Learning to Make Decisions

The second classroom approach to moral education is the
Debate Strategy. Its primary objective is to provide students
with direct experience in taking and defending positions on
moral issues. The Debate Strategy has been used successfully
for centuries (medieval moral theologians called it casuistry—
the art of applying general ethical principles to specific cases)
on the presumption that experience is the best teacher, or that
practice in decision-making increases one's skills.

More recently, this strategy has acquired a new rationale.
Harvard psychologist Lawrence Kohlberg's theory of moral
development suggests that, over a period of time, people move
from one moral orientation or state to a higher one when
they're challenged by problems they have difficulty answering
and are attracted by the reasons offered by a higher-stage
orientation.* The educational implication here is that if young
people are presented with case problems or moral dilemmas for
debate, this experience will facilitate their development toward
mature moral thinking.

The debate approach has proven very effective. It's also
relatively simple: The teacher gives the students an account of
an actual or hypothetical case involving a specific problem or
problems, and then asks the students what they would do if
they found themselves in that situation. If the case is a good
one, students will disagree about what should be done. Once
this disagreement is established, the students are divided into
two or more groups according to their opinions and given a few
minutes to share, formulate, and develop the reasons for their
decisions. After they've had time to do this, full class discussion
is resumed, and the groups on each side of the issue are given

*Professor Kohlberg's theories have dominated the field of moral education in the
United States for almost a decade. See Moral Education in Theory and Practice,
Chapter 6, for an account and criticism of his theories.

the opportunity to state and defend the reasons for the choices they made, or to criticize the reasons given by the other group(s).

Case problems can be presented for class debate in many ways, including role play, film videotape, or oral presentation. Often, they're most effective if they're just written on the chalkboard, or if copies are made for each student; this gives participants a chance to absorb the details at their own rate and allows them to refer back to the problem to clarify questions they may have. In oral presentations alone, important points are often entirely neglected, and the teacher may find it necessary to draw attention to them later; this almost always detracts from the student-centered discussion.

Example:

A GHOST FROM THE PAST

George, a friend of yours, has come to you for advice. He has been going with Jane for almost a year; they've grown to love each other very much, and they plan to be married in six months.

George's problem is that about seven years ago he was arrested for breaking into a radio store with some friends and served three months in jail. He says that since that time he's "gone straight." He's now held a responsible job for three years, and feels that he's learned his lesson and his life has changed.

George is afraid to tell Jane about his prison record. He fears that she won't understand; he also worries that her parents, who have only reluctantly accepted him, will find out and do something to stop the wedding. On the other hand, he wonders whether he should get married without being completely open and honest with Jane and telling her all about it.

Would you advise George to tell Jane about his past?

Example:

GUARD DUTY

You're a sergeant in the army, and your country is at war. You've been put in charge of sixteen prisoners of war who haven't yet been moved to a camp.

Your side begins to lose ground in a particular area, and it's obvious that you'll have to retreat soon. The enemy is advancing more quickly than you've expected, and the situation is getting desperate. You can't just leave the prisoners, and you don't have enough time to bring them along.

As you're about to pull out, you receive orders from your superior to shoot the prisoners rather than let them escape.

Would you shoot them?

Case problems can be written on nearly every topic—from the common (Would you give back the money if you received too much change at the supermarket?) to the unusual (If you were a jury member and found a defendant guilty of murder, would you recommend the death penalty?), and from history (If you had been President Truman, what would you have decided about using the atomic bomb?) to the present (If you were one of Karen Ann Quinlan's parents, would you have removed her medical life-support systems?).

Many teachers develop their own free-flowing styles for using the Debate Strategy, while others follow a more formal model. One good model has been developed by Ronald E. Galbraith and Thomas M. Jones.* A version of this model, which was developed at the Carnegie-Mellon Moral Education Project, has also been incorporated into the Holt Rinehart secondary social studies series texts on American Studies.

The Debate Strategy: A Suggested Approach

The general lesson plan for the Debate Strategy can be relatively simple. The following step-by-step procedure is suggested:

1. Present the case to the class. This can be accomplished in a number of ways; those which are usually

---

*Ronald E. Galbraith and Thomas M. Jones, Moral Reasoning: A Teaching Handbook for Adapting Kohlberg to the Classroom. Anoka, Minn: Greenhaven Press, 1976.

considered preferable include either writing the case on the chalkboard or photocopying it and passing it out to the students. Either of these approaches allows students to read the case themselves, absorb the facts at their own rate, and refer back to it if they have questions later on in the discussion.

2.   Give the students a few minutes to think about the case and begin to formulate their opinions. Don't allow any discussion yet—this time should be used to let students make up their own minds. Ask for a show of hands on various opinions—on "yes" or "no," for example, or on "I would" or "I wouldn't."

3.   Divide the class into small groups for discussion purposes. Have students gather into small groups according to opinions they hold in common. It's best to keep group size to eight or fewer so that everyone in a group will have the chance to discuss his or her feelings about the case.

Allow five to ten minutes for the small-group discussions. Instruct the groups to talk about their opinions together and to be prepared to state their best reasons for their decisions.

If nearly everyone in the class holds a common viewpoint, there probably won't be enough differences of opinion to facilitate a good debate. If and when this occurs, you can either (a) alter the facts of the case so that some students will change their opinions, or (b) discuss the case briefly as a class and then move on to another, more controversial one.

4.   Bring the class together again to discuss and debate the issue. Give each side the opportunity to state the reasons for their decisions and to answer the questions posed by the other side. Try to probe all the consequences of the various choices made.

Probe questions play an important part in moving the class discussion out of the argument context and into a more effective developmental one. These may include, for example:

•   clarifying questions, which ask students to define terms or clarify opinions; e.g., "What do you mean by 'unfair'?" "Why is loyalty important?"

•   value focus questions, which ask students to identify and define their value commitments; e.g., "Is keeping a promise the most important thing in this case?"

- value conflict questions; e.g., "Which is more important here—loyalty to a friend, or obedience to the law?"
- role-switch questions, which force students to put themselves in another's shoes; e.g., "What if you were George's fiancée? Would you want to know the truth?"
- universalizing questions; e.g., "Is it ever right to do...?" or "Is it always right to do...?" The probe questions, as Barry Beyer explains,

> ...require students to do a number of things which seem to facilitate movement from the lower to the higher stages of moral reasoning—(1) to think in increasingly more generalizable terms, (2) to develop an increasingly broad social perspective, (3) to develop an ability to see and empathize with more than one side of an issue, and (4) to focus increasingly on the larger moral issues implicit in a moral dilemma.*

5. Bring the discussion to a close. Summarize the best reasons for and against each opinion in the case. Ask students to reconsider and change their decisions if they wish, or to write out their final decisions and reasons.

Most teachers, after one or two trial runs, are able to use the Debate Strategy in this form quite easily and effectively.

Writing Case Problems: Adding Your Own Dimension to the Debate Strategy

Many teachers prefer writing their own case problems to suit their classes' needs and situations. Generally, it's best to keep cases simple enough that the issue may be easily grasped. It helps to include enough description (for example, by giving the principal characters' names) to make the case sound real, however. It's also important to make sure that cases contain issues which the students themselves actually see as problems. In order to be effective, cases must stimulate students on their

---

*Barry K. Beyer, "Conducting Moral Discussions in the Classroom"; mimeographed paper, 1976. The five types of probe questions mentioned in this section are drawn from Beyer's account of the debate strategy.

level—which isn't necessarily the same as the adult level. The younger the students are, the more important this is. This consideration can be balanced, though, by the realization that students can be brought to see issues and problems which they haven't really thought about before. After all, raising students' consciousness of moral problems is one of the aims of moral education.

One way of raising students' awareness of a situation so that they can recognize it as a moral problem is by scheduling a formal debate. This can be accomplished by assigning students to two teams and allowing them time to research the subject before the debate. This method is especially effective in courses involving complex social and legal problems (for example, Should the law allow courts to order the sterilization of mentally ill or retarded people if their condition can be inherited by their children?).

A third point crucial to writing good cases involves making sure that they pose clear "yes" or "no" questions, or set the stage for eliciting other strongly opposite opinions. "Should John call the police, or not?" will result in either of two responses and thus create two clear sides for the debate. A question like, "What should John do?" aims at an entirely different decision-making skill (this is the focus of the Rational Strategy; see pages 43-50); it may elicit several different responses and result in interaction that's far too complicated for a clear debate.

Cases can, of course, be either real (that is, drawn from actual circumstances) or hypothetical (the teacher can simply make them up). A teacher need not feel that he or she has to discuss controversial social issues. Some teachers have the misguided notion that moral education is all a matter of telling students the teacher's opinions about premarital sex, abortion, drug use, or some other problem; this can defeat the whole purpose of the moral discussion. If the teacher wants to deal with actual decision-making, it might be best to avoid issues on which students are likely to have well-established opinions. Teachers will have to look carefully at their students, the school, and the community as they develop materials and adapt them for use in the classroom. There may be situations in which it would be better to skirt controversial issues entirely.

Facilitating Classroom Interaction: Getting the Ball Rolling

The success of the Debate Strategy depends on student participation. Many teachers are reluctant or uncomfortable about using student-centered strategies precisely because of this fact. With teacher-centered strategies, such as lectures, texts, tests, workbooks, and the like, the class can go on regardless of whether students participate; a lecture can still be given even if students sleep all the way through it. With student-centered strategies, however, the teacher must be willing to give up the security of having everything "under control." If a teacher presents a case for debate, for example, and the students themselves don't feel that there's a moral or a decision-making issue in it, they'll all simply answer "yes" or "no," and the strategy may seem to fall on its face. There's really no educational problem with this sort of "failure," though; when something doesn't work in class, the teacher at least knows that it's because it isn't on the students' level or because they're not interested in it or don't see it as important. When a lecture isn't on the students' level, however, there may be no such feedback, and the class stays "under control" whether or not any real education is going on.

A "breakdown" in this strategy is really only a temporary malfunction—a built-in criterion of educational effectiveness which tells the teacher that it's time to shift to an alternative approach. Galbraith and Jones have developed an effective remedy for this negative feedback situation in the model they have proposed for teaching moral dilemmas. When writing a case, they suggest, teachers should also consider further information or possible changes in the details which they can add to the case if needed; in other words, they should be prepared to alter the case to make an unpopular choice attractive to a greater number of students. If the students all respond to a case by saying, for example, "Yes, the President should be impeached," the teacher may want to add an optional detail—perhaps the fact that the country is in the midst of a foreign crisis about which the Vice President is ill informed. This addition should serve to change some students' minds and get the discussion off the ground. If the teacher is prepared to offer alternatives like these, a real debate may result from what first appeared to be a failure.

Another way of stimulating differences of opinion among students is to offer some good reason for accepting the choice that the majority has rejected. If, for example, a class is given a case in which a boy's dog is killed and the parents are wondering whether to tell him about it, the majority opinion may be, "No, they shouldn't tell him." The teacher might then suggest, "Well, if they don't tell him, the boy may resent it and refuse to believe anything else his parents tell him," or ask the students, "What if this makes him think that his parents never tell him about important things that happen? What if he stopped trusting his parents because of this?" Tactics like these may revive the case—or they may not.

These two methods of stimulating student response—adding details, and playing the devil's advocate—may indeed make cases more interesting and result in more stimulating discussions, but they aren't foolproof. When the outcome of a teacher's attempts to encourage student discussion seems questionable, it's better to leave the case behind than to belabor it. Sometimes, cases can be changed easily, or good reasons for unpopular opinions can attract support, but if student interest isn't obviously aroused it's better to go onto another case or another strategy altogether.

It's nearly impossible to predict how long students' attention and interest will be held by a case problem. In some instances, they may spend an entire class profitably on one minor point, or they may go back to a case discussed some days earlier and raise the whole issue again. Although the results of situations like these are difficult to assess, students do seem to learn a great deal from this kind of replay, much as some people learn from videotape analysis. At any rate, a teacher shouldn't insist on pursuing a case that simply isn't working; moving on to the next activity (this means having more than one prepared) is often the best remedy. Here again, the class atmosphere is important. If students know that the teacher respects their opinions and is attempting to present them with materials that correspond to their interests, they probably won't mind when he or she drops a case or strategy which doesn't work. After all, a teacher shows more respect for students' opinions by accepting their feedback judgment and going on to the next topic than by attempting to force them into an activity they're not interested in. All too often, a teacher is more self-conscious than the students when it comes to admitting failure.

Whether or not a teacher should take part in a classroom debate also depends on the educational atmosphere that exists. If it's one in which students are unwilling to offer opinions contrary to those given (or implied) by the teacher, the teacher should keep out of the discussion even when asked to participate. The Debate Strategy, when properly implemented, places the teacher in the role of impartial facilitator, and this actually makes it easy for him or her to avoid influencing the discussion with personal opinions. The ideal atmosphere, of course, is one in which students respect and consider the teacher's opinions while feeling free to express their own views, knowing that they'll be challenged to give good reasons for their decisions. Teachers who make a genuine effort to maintain the distinction between expressing their views and imposing them can usually work out a comfortable style of interaction.

There are times when students are genuinely puzzled and look for help. Sometimes, direct assistance from the teacher is good; at other times, the teacher may find it best to let students work out a problem on their own. Much depends on how puzzled the students are, how insecure they feel when they're unable to make up their minds, and how unlikely it is that they'll be able to resolve the issue without any guidance at all. A moral debate isn't effective when it results in students feeling confused and overly disturbed; this can result in their being reluctant to participate in future discussions, and can make the task of moral education even more difficult than it sometimes is.

Using the Chalkboard

Once students have become accustomed to this teaching model, it's often helpful to keep a chalkboard account of each debate. Either the teacher or a student can be responsible for writing the case question on the board and dividing the space into "Pro" and "Con" or "Yes" and "No" sides, each with two columns: one for reasons, and one for criticisms of these reasons.

Example: Question: If you were given too much change at the supermarket, would you return the extra money to the cashier?

Yes

Reasons	Criticisms
She might call the police.	The police couldn't arrest you or prove anything.
You'd feel guilty.	You'd get over it after a while.
It isn't your money.	The store can afford it.

No

Reasons	Criticisms
Stores overcharge anyway.	The cashier will have to pay it back herself.
Finders keepers.	Sometimes it's illegal to keep things you find.
It was the cashier's mistake.	People make mistakes— why not help her out?
The store won't miss it.	Stores make up the costs of mistakes and shoplifting by charging everyone more.

The chalkboard record should not, of course, be allowed to interfere with or become more important than the actual debate. It can, however, be an effective device for both summing up issues and reminding students of the facts of the case and the resulting conflicts. This technique can be especially useful if the teacher concludes the session by asking students to write a paragraph defending one side or the other. As an awareness activity for building empathy, students can be asked to write a paragraph expressing the best reason given for the other side's opinion.

Chapter 4:
The Rational Strategy: Learning to Recognize Alternatives and Foresee Consequences

Like the Debate Strategy, the Rational Strategy presents case problems for class discussion. The educational objectives and classroom interaction of the two methods are very different, however. While the debate approach emphasizes forming and defending a single opinion—pro or con, yes or no—the rational approach aims at developing the specific skills of looking for alternative courses of action and foreseeing the consequences of those actions.

In practice, the Debate Strategy and the Rational Strategy complement each other in many ways. During a debate, students are asked to make decisions and then defend their decisions by giving reasons for them. They learn to speak their minds and publicly affirm their choices. The rational approach, on the other hand, asks students to withhold judgment—to not make decisions—until they've considered several different approaches to the problem and the consequences of each. This strategy, then, is more likely to leave students with the impression that decision-making is an intellectual or rational process which people can do well or poorly, rather than encouraging them—as the Debate Strategy sometimes does—to feel that decisions are basically products of feelings. The debate format presents students with alternatives from which to choose; the rational format asks students to come up with their own alternatives and consider the possible results of their choices.

Decision-making skills are of great importance to mature moral development. It's often been said that young people tend to make poor decisions simply because they don't stop to think about the possible consequences of their actions. It's certainly true that people often don't make good choices because such choices never occur to them. Discovering alternatives is an imaginative task, and the imagination plays a crucial role in moral thought and decision-making. When people complain that others don't "think" before acting, what they're really criticizing is their lack of development and use of rational skills.

"What If...But Then...": A Useful First Step

Drawing attention to alternative decisions and their consequences generally runs contrary to students' immediate impulses to make quick decisions. It's possible to do this before getting into the Rational Strategy itself, however—it's possible to set the stage, in other words—by means of a discussion technique which emphasizes this aspect of decision-making by ruling out quick judgments.

The technique is simple: A very brief problem is stated, in a single sentence if possible (a previously discussed case problem can be used, too, although it should now be stated as an open-ended question rather than an either/or choice), and students are asked to respond to it.

Example: A sergeant is asked to execute prisoners of war. What should he do?

When faced with making a decision about the atomic bomb, what could President Truman have done?

If a teacher catches a third-grade student stealing pencils, what can the teacher do?

The students' response is somewhat controlled in that they're allowed to make only two kinds of statements:

1. "What if..." statements, which propose an alternative course of action; or

2. "But then..." statements, which respond to the "What if..." statements by discussing some of the possible consequences.

Since neither of these types of statements constitutes an actual decision on the matter, and none of the statements has to be defended by reasons, the whole interaction consists of thinking up alternatives and predicting their consequences. Because this technique has a sort of brainstorming effect, some of the general rules of brainstorming might be helpful:

- All ideas are acceptable;
- Say whatever comes into your head;
- Keep the discussion moving quickly (someone can keep a record of contributions to see who makes the most);
- Let other people's statements lead you to new ideas; and
- It's okay to repeat an earlier idea.

The discussion may last for only a few minutes, or it may go on for some time. Again, there's no way to predict whether students will have many ideas about a problem or will run out of alternatives and consequences rather quickly. It may take a trial run or two before students will catch on to the rules; as with most games, they'll probably jump in and stop someone who forgets the rules. It's best to prepare four, five, or even more topic questions ahead of time, even for a brief session, since there's little profit in attempting to do anything with questions which elicit few responses.

Moving into the Rational Strategy

It's relatively easy to move from the "What if...But then..." exercise into the Rational Strategy. The teacher simply presents a more elaborate moral dilemma and then slows down the discussion of alternatives and consequences by writing them on the chalkboard. It's important to keep in mind that the essence of the Rational Strategy is to require students to take a careful look at all of the alternatives and consequences a particular problem suggests.

Students who are accustomed to the Debate Strategy can usually adapt to the rational approach without too much difficulty. The basic difference between the two will become apparent to them when the teacher announces that he or she wants the class to consider a problem without trying to make an immediate decision about it, and then presents a case which asks them what a person should do rather than insisting on a yes or no choice.

Although the issues which naturally lend themselves to the Rational Strategy are those in which it's obvious that a number of alternatives exist, case problems are written in basically the same way as for the Debate Strategy. The essential difference between the two is that the Debate Strategy requires a definite pro or con response, while the Rational Strategy leaves the final question open-ended.

Example:

HIT AND RUN

Dan, a close friend of yours, drives up to your house one evening while you're outside. As he gets out of his car, you can see that he's been drinking and appears to be very upset. He tells you that while he was driving on a back road to your house, he sideswiped a girl on a bicycle. He looked in his mirror and saw that the girl had fallen, but he was frightened, especially since he'd been drinking, and didn't stop to see if she was hurt. No one else was on the road at the time, and Dan feels sure that his car couldn't be identified. He asks you what he should do.

What will you say?

Example:

LOST AND FOUND

Gregg was walking past a bank in the downtown area one afternoon when he saw an elderly woman who had just come out of the bank drop a brown envelope onto the sidewalk. By the time he got over to where she had dropped it, the woman had crossed the street and disappeared into a department store. Gregg picked up the envelope—which had already been opened— and looked inside. It contained $375, and was addressed to Mrs. Elsie Jordan. Gregg recognized the address as being in a poorer section of the city. The return address was that of the Railroad Pension Fund in Pittsburgh.

What should Gregg do?

The Rational Strategy can be used to stimulate discussion among the class as a whole, and it's perhaps best to introduce

 ©Winston Press, Inc. Permission is given to reproduce this page for student use.

the strategy by doing at least one case in this way. Once students have learned the basics of the strategy, however, it's much more effective to divide the class into small discussion groups of no more than three or four members. This approach involves more students in actually attempting to think of alternatives and consequences than is possible in a large group. How much students actually learn and grow depends on the amount of practice they get in thinking about moral problems.

The procedure is the same whether it's aimed at a whole class discussion or small groups. First, students are presented with a specific case. Next, they're asked to list all of the alternatives open to the person in the case. Finally, they're requested to choose three or four alternatives which seem best and then describe to the rest of the class the consequences of each.

The teacher may not agree with all of the alternatives suggested; some will be outrageous, and the teacher should feel free to say so. If the emphasis is on imagining alternatives, though—as it should be—the teacher should exercise some restraint. Suggestions that come up in a brainstorming atmosphere must not be simply squelched, or students will get the impression that only "proper" suggestions are acceptable. Some suggestions may seem silly—for example, Dan's friend could advise him to skip town, or Gregg could put the money back in the envelope and leave it on the street. The teacher can only hope that the outrageous or silly suggestions will be eliminated during the class discussion, and continue to express his or her personal objections if they aren't. When the atmosphere is right, students will feel free to suggest many alternatives without feeling intimidated by the teacher. It's essential to stress that the acceptance of an alternative doesn't necessarily imply approval, however.

A record of alternatives and consequences should be kept on the chalkboard or on student worksheets so that the various alternatives can be compared and discussed without too much confusion. Almost any format can be used for the worksheets as long as the various alternatives and their consequences can be grouped together for easy reference and comparison. An example of a worksheet follows. The teacher may simply duplicate it on the chalkboard or make a copy for each student.

RATIONAL STRATEGY WORKSHEET

Problem: _____

Alternative 1.

_____

Consequences _____

_____

_____

Alternative 2.

_____

Consequences _____

_____

_____

Alternative 3.

_____

Consequences _____

_____

_____

©Winston Press, Inc. Permission is given to reproduce this page for student use.

The worksheet can be especially helpful in small-group discussions because it gives students a clear indication of just what they're expected to produce. Since the same worksheet format can be used for many different types of case problem discussions, students who use it regularly will become accustomed to it, and it will lose some of its mystique and become more of a tool. With practice, students will get much quicker at thinking up alternatives and spotting the consequences. One hopes, of course, that they'll also develop a tendency to look at daily decisions, especially moral issues, from a similarly rational perspective. In any case, teaching them how to do it and giving them practice in it are important steps in the direction of stimulating moral growth.

The number of possible alternatives and consequences should never be limited ahead of time. Students should be encouraged to use extra paper or more than one worksheet if needed, and to look at all possibilities regardless of how ridiculous they may seem. The brainstorming atmosphere should be maintained for the duration of the discussion. An alternative which one group of students rejects may prove attractive to another group; similarly, an alternative which seems out of the question at first can look much more attractive after the consequences of other alternatives have been considered. This, in a nutshell, is the point of this particular strategy: The more the students are encouraged to use their heads, the more they're apt to learn from this strategy.

Some of the same consequences may appear under more than one alternative heading; again, brainstorming all possible consequences is an essential part of this approach. If extremely unlikely consequences are mentioned, they can be enclosed in parentheses as an indication that they shouldn't be taken too seriously.

After the worksheets have been filled in or the chalkboard list is fairly complete, students can be asked to review the consequences of each alternative and place a plus sign before those which are "good," or beneficial, and a minus sign before those which are "bad," or detrimental. Or summaries of the reports from each group can be written on the chalkboard and the plus and minus signs can be added at this time, rather than during the small-group sessions, if this seems preferable.

Finally, the problem of actually making a decision shouldn't be avoided or ignored. Often, it's more difficult to come to a decision after considering the alternatives and consequences than it is before doing so; arriving at a decision is still important, however. Some discussion questions can help, like the following:

- Which consequence under each alternative seems most important?
- Out of these, which consequence seems most important of all?
- If it's a plus consequence, is this the alternative you would choose if you were making the decision?
- If it's a minus consequence, would you eliminate that alternative entirely?
- Which alternative would you choose if you were the person in the case who had to make the decision?

Students may agree on this final choice, or they may not. If they do, the teacher may wish to move to a discussion of the values involved (see the Concept Strategy, pages 51-76). If there is significant disagreement about which choice is the best one, and if the students are still sufficiently interested in the problem, the teacher may wish to move to a Debate Strategy. An informal debate is better than a formal one at this point, though, since students will already have considered the case at some length.

Once the discussion has gone as far as it can go, asking students to write a paragraph stating their own decisions and their reasons for them can be an effective way to conclude this approach.

Chapter 5:
The Concept Strategy:
A Way of Understanding Our World

The fourth strategy for moral education focuses on the concepts normally used by people in our society when making decisions and reasoning about them. Consider, for example, the following statements:

If his conscience is going to bother him that much, he shouldn't do it.

She has a right to say what she thinks.

It wouldn't be fair for him to have the car all of the time.

She isn't old enough to take on that sort of responsibility.

It would be nice if he offered to help, but I wouldn't call it a duty.

Each of these statements contains a concept—conscience, right, fairness, responsibility, duty—which is often used to describe the morality of a certain decision or action. These concepts (and many more) are considered by most people in our society to be so basic that they're used in all types of situations by persons of many different moral perspectives. Although there's a great deal of disagreement concerning what rights, duties, or responsibilities human beings have—or should have—, people who consider life from any type of moral perspective are apt to use these terms. These concepts and others like them have been incorporated into our vocabularies so thoroughly that they're almost unavoidable. Because they're so all-pervasive, helping young people to develop a sense of what these words mean and how they're used is one way of teaching them to look at human situations from a moral point of view.

Now consider the following statements:

Honesty is the best policy.

A friend in need is a friend indeed.

She deserves a fair trial.

No taxation without representation.

All men are created equal.

These statements also include concepts which are commonly heard in moral discussions—honesty, friendship, justice, the right to vote (suffrage), and equality. These terms, though, don't refer to aspects of moral thought as such, but to specific social values which are prevalent throughout most of Western society. They're generally recognized as values which should be considered whenever decisions are made on social issues. People appeal to honesty or friendship, for example, when they're attempting to justify their own actions to others, or when they're trying to convince someone that a certain action is the right one to take in a specific situation. Justice, equality, and the right to vote, on the other hand, are social values which are considered so fundamental that they've been incorporated into the Constitution and the laws of the United States, and have thus become legal rights as well as moral values.

A solid understanding of these concepts—whether or not one agrees with any particular interpretation of them—is crucial to moral growth. Personal and public discussions of moral issues can influence the kinds of decisions we make, perhaps more than we care to admit, because we're usually concerned about being able to justify our actions to others. Morality, then, is almost always a social matter. Understanding other people's values and recognizing which ones occupy official places in our society are necessary skills if one aims at comprehending how our world works and what's expected of the people in it. Thus, an important goal for moral education is to help students develop these skills.

Developing one's own values is the focus of the Awareness Strategy (pages 23-32); the Concept Strategy brings this awareness into its full social context. Values don't simply spring up out of an individual's feelings, nor are lifestyles invented in isolation; rather, each of us is born into a particular society which contains both a rich cultural tradition of values and a limited number of lifestyles. Attaining moral maturity requires one to grow up to find his or her own values and lifestyle within this social and cultural framework. This is true regardless of the environment one is born into; although particular values and lifestyles may be different from place to place or from country to country, moral education always presumes the existence of some cultural pattern.

In considering this goal of moral education—helping young people to develop an awareness of values and how those values relate to the world around them—we need to keep the middle way in mind at all times (see pages 14-16). We must be sure to avoid indoctrination. If we insist on presenting or teaching one set of social values as moral "absolutes," or give students the impression that these values constitute unbending moral "rules," we'll be guilty of doing precisely what we should try our best to avoid. It's important to teach moral concepts and social values because doing so helps moral education to avoid the dangers of relativism; when we move too far in the direction of absolutism, however, we take risks that are equally great and self-defeating.

The moral eduation teacher can avoid absolutism by reminding himself or herself of two important points: that the teaching of value concepts must always be objective, never subjective; and that concepts themselves are by nature both vague and complex. The first consideration simply means that the teacher should keep his or her own set of values out of the moral discussion entirely. Instead, he or she should be familiar with the values commonly held by people in Western culture and in American society as part of that culture. He or she must also have a working knowledge of the values embodied in the history and documents of Western civilization and our particular society. (Even though the moral educator in a private or parochial school or religious education program will also be responsible for presenting these concepts with an eye toward the moral perspective of a particular religious tradition, he or she should still be aware that these concepts generally include a variety of interpretations.) In short, we must be willing to convey the impression that we're trying to give students a picture of the values held by people in our society which make that society what it is, not that we're trying to convince them that these values are always right and never subject to reform or criticism.

Moral educators should, of course, help students to develop their own value commitments, and it's hoped that this can be at least partially accomplished by teaching them about the values common in our society and its history. We deny their rights as human beings, however, when we present these values as standards to which they're expected to conform.

The second defense against absolutism or indoctrination has to do with the nature of value concepts themselves. Defining a "concept" as such can be a difficult if not impossible task. First of all, a concept isn't a word (the word only represents the concept), nor is it a material object. Rather, it's a mental image of some sort which stands for or represents a whole collection of objects, ideas, and feelings. A concept, then, may be looked upon as a sort of set (to use a mathematical term) of mental images which have something in common.

Think for a moment about the concept dog. It may bring to mind a picture of a specific dog—such as a family pet, or a neighbor's dog that's a particular nuisance—, but when one stops to think about the word, and from there moves to a consideration of the concept of dog, one realizes that it encompasses not only a variety of different breeds but also a number of ideas which may not have anything at all to do with a specific dog or type of dog.

Now imagine the concept chair. Perhaps you envision an easy chair and then a rocking chair. Already you've replaced one specific set of characteristics—what you imagine an easy chair to look like—with another. An easy chair may have four legs, while a rocking chair may have two rockers. An easy chair may be upholstered, while a rocking chair may not be. It should be apparent that what one person—you—means by the word chair might not be at all what another person means by it. Nor, of course, can any two individuals' concepts of a particular object or idea be exactly the same. At the very least, then, a person must progress through a whole series of mental images before he or she can even begin to capture the essence of any one concept.

The two examples above—dog and chair—are fairly simple ones. We're aided in our understanding of them by two things: our imaginations, and our society's definitions of these concepts. In America, a dog is never a cat, and a chair is never a refrigerator. While it may seem as if the interpretations of a particular concept or word are never-ending, we can take comfort in the fact that our society and our understanding of that society does impose certain limitations on what a specific concept can and can't entail.

These limitations more often apply to our concepts of concrete objects or things than to our concepts of abstract realities, however, and this is where moral education can become quite complicated. Consider, for example, what's meant by the word revolution. There are revolutionary wars and industrial revolutions and cultural revolutions. There are political and social revolutions, peaceful ones and bloody ones. In addition, there's the revolution that the earth makes around the sun. Are these all parts of the same concept, or not?

Even the concept of concept is difficult to define or describe. In addition to being vague and general, concepts are often highly personal. In his book Thinking With Concepts, John Wilson addresses this problem by saying,

> There is, strictly speaking, no such thing as "the" concept of a thing. When we talk, in a kind of shorthand, about "the" meaning of a word, we refer to those significant elements in all the many and various usages of the word which make the word comprehensible....
>
> In the same way when we talk of "the" concept of a thing, we are often referring in an abbreviated way to all the different concepts of that thing which individual people have, and to the extent to which these concepts coincide. Thus we can talk about "the" concept of justice entertained by the ancient Romans; but also we can talk about your concept of justice, or my concept, or Cicero's concept, just as we often say, "His idea of justice is so-and-so." We must not, in any case, imagine that "the" concept of a thing is a separate entity on its own.*

Avoiding indoctrination and absolutism when teaching value concepts shouldn't be at all difficult, because concepts themselves are so very broad and general. When we're dealing with something we can barely begin to define or comprehend, we certainly can't presume to teach it as a specific moral rule or standard. If we accept this definition of the nature of

*John Wilson, Thinking With Concepts. Cambridge, England: Cambridge University Press, 1971, p. 54.

concepts, we no longer have to worry about the dangers of teaching definite codes when we attempt to teach values. When we accurately—that is, objectively—convey value concepts to students, we'll be helping them to understand that values are interpreted differently by different people under different circumstances. In other words, we'll be saying that students have to be responsible for considering these different interpretations when trying to come up with their own. This consciousness of the possible variations on the same themes, and the subsequent development of personal opinions and values, is what moral growth is all about.

Moving into the Concept Strategy

Any strategy for teaching value concepts should reflect this understanding of what a concept both is and isn't. As Barry Beyer has said,

> Concepts cannot be given or told to anyone—at least not beyond the level of simple recognition, anyway. We must develop our own concept of something if it is to become a useful part of our cognitive library....Teaching concepts...really means putting students into learning experiences that will facilitate their own conceptualization about a given concept.*

The Concept Strategy, then, attempts to do precisely that. As offered here, it has three parts: <u>Explanation</u>, <u>Identification</u>, and <u>Modeling</u>.

Explanation: Introducing the Concept

The first step of this strategy is, of course, that of selecting a particular concept to be approached in the classroom. The teacher should then be prepared to give a brief introduction of the concept to the class by naming it, supplying a dictionary

---

*"Teaching Concepts in the Classroom" in Barry K. Beyer and Anthony N. Penna, eds., Concepts in the Social Studies. Washington, D.C.: National Council for the Social Studies, 1971, p. 61. Reprinted from Barry K. Beyer, Inquiry in the Social Studies Classroom: A Strategy for Teaching. Columbus, Ohio: Charles E. Merrill Publishing Co., 1971.

definition for it, and proving both examples and counter-examples, or opposites, of it. This process won't usually require much time, since the nature of concepts makes any type of explanation in and of itself insufficient. So the teacher should introduce a concept to the class briefly, in much the same way he or she would introduce a new student.

Some teachers assume that once something is explained it has been, or can be, learned. This isn't the case—especially with value concepts; they must be used, applied, corrected, investigated, and often lived with for a while before they acquire the complex sense they merit (just as a new student can never be "learned" via the teacher's introduction alone). A basic explanation or description with examples and counter-examples is, however, a necessary first step in this strategy.

Example: The dictionary defines peace as the absence of war or hostilities. Countries make agreements with one another and sign "peace treaties." We are fortunate to live in an age of peace; and people almost always want to live in peace, but sometimes they feel they have strong reasons to go to war [a counter-example].

Some people say that a country isn't at peace, even though it isn't at war, when people in that country are oppressed or denied their rights. For example, many would not say that South Africa was at peace now, even though it isn't at war.

Other people think of peace as meaning a kind of inner contentment—such as "peace of mind," or "Shalom," meaning "peace," which Jewish people use as a greeting.

Identification: Clarifying the Concept

The second part of the Concept Strategy is closely related to the Debate and Rational Strategies (see pages 33-50) and to some Awareness Activities (see pages 23-32).

Once a value concept is introduced, case problems which have been discussed previously can be re-examined as possible examples of the concept. In fact, once some value concepts have been introduced to a class via either the Debate Strategy or the

Rational Strategy, the teacher may find it an easy matter to add concept identification as a supplementary "level" to either strategy. Identification is simply recognition of the values at stake in a particular discussion. Thus, for each possible decision pro or con during a debate, and for each separate alternative mentioned during a Rational Strategy exercise, it should be possible for students to identify both the values upheld and the values denied. (There may be more than one of each, and the same value may appear in more than one place—even on both sides of a debate.) This identifying may be done on the chalkboard at the end of a debate by isolating the values upheld and denied in both the pro and con columns; or, for the Rational Strategy approach, spaces for it may be incorporated into the worksheet. The expanded chalkboard or worksheet outlines could take the forms given on pages 59-61.

In teaching value concepts, it's important to encourage students to identify a number of different cases as involving the same value or values. This will probably happen when the teacher arranges a series of case problems, along with other materials in a relevant study unit, for the teaching of a particular value concept.

Whether a particular value is upheld or denied in a given answer to a problem isn't the focus here; what is essential is that a specific value is involved, and that students see the problem as a question of this value. The particular value that's the focus of attention for a specific unit or case may often end up in the Values Denied column in other instances. Again, the aim of this strategy is not to teach young people that certain values, whatever they may be, can never be overriden or criticized; the fact that they can be is important to the students' understanding of any value. Some people, for example, might feel that the value of the freedom of the press can be overriden by the value of national security. This opinion illustrates the value concept just as well as does the opinion of a person who upholds the freedom of the press during the same discussion.

When a number of cases involving the same value or values are reviewed together, a summary outline or worksheet will help to illustrate the common values involved. The following summary outline shows a situation in which the first

DEBATE STRATEGY—VALUES IDENTIFICATION WORKSHEET

Problem: _____

Reasons Pro

_____

_____

_____

_____

Values Upheld

_____

_____

Values Denied

_____

_____

Reasons Con

_____

_____

_____

_____

Values Upheld

_____

_____

Values Denied

_____

_____

©Winston Press, Inc. Permission is given to reproduce this page for student use.

RATIONAL STRATEGY—VALUES IDENTIFICATION WORKSHEET

Problem: _____

Alternative 1.

_____

Consequences

_____

_____

_____

Values Upheld

_____

_____

_____

Values Denied

_____

_____

_____

Alternative 2.

_____

Consequences

_____

_____

_____

Values Upheld

_____

_____

_____

Values Denied

_____

_____

_____

Alternative 3.

_____

Consequences

_____

_____

_____

Values Upheld

_____

_____

_____

Values Denied

_____

_____

_____

problem was discussed according to the Debate Strategy and the second according to the Rational Strategy.

 Example:

VALUE IDENTIFICATION SUMMARY WORKSHEET

Cases	Decision	Major Value Upheld	Major Value Denied
1. _____	Pro _____	_____	_____
	Con_____	_____	_____
	Alternatives		
2. _____	(A) _____	_____	_____
	(B) _____	_____	_____
	(C) _____	_____	_____

Modeling: Expanding and Illustrating the Concept

The third aspect of the Concept Strategy attempts to convey the understanding of a value concept in all of its complexity by means of a diagram or model of the mental image.* The model is, of course, merely an effort to convey a notion which can't be precisely defined; it should, however, help the student to construct a similar understanding or image for himself or herself. There is, therefore, no "right" form for a model, nor is there an absolutely correct or incorrect answer to any of the various questions which serve to draw attention to the different aspects of a value concept.

The diagram which follows illustrates the basic outline for a value concept model. It can be used as a chalkboard outline or, after students have become familiar with it, as a worksheet for small group discussions or individual evaluations.

*I am indebted to Professor Barry K. Beyer for the suggestion of this general approach, and would recommend his book, Inquiry in the Social Studies Classroom: A Strategy for Teachers. Columbus, Ohio: Charles E. Merrill, 1971. Of course, Professor Beyer is not responsible for my development of his general approach for the purpose of teaching value concepts.

CONCEPT STRATEGY WORKSHEET

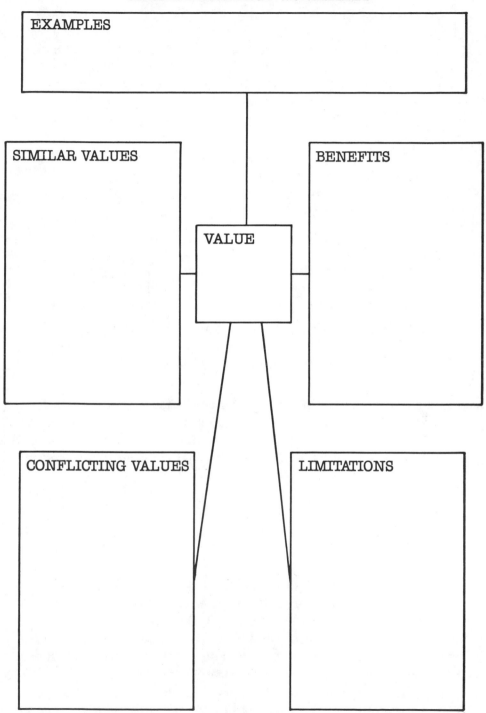

EXAMPLES

SIMILAR VALUES

BENEFITS

VALUE

CONFLICTING VALUES

LIMITATIONS

©Winston Press, Inc. Permission is given to reproduce this page for student use. **63**

```
┌──────────┐
│ VALUE    │
└──────────┘
```

The value concept itself occupies the central box in this model.
It is signified by the word commonly used to designate, or
name, the value. This central box is a good place to write the
brief Explanation of the value, as discussed above; this can
be a dictionary definition or simply an indication of the area of
human life to which the value refers.

      The illustrations which follow include concepts and
language appropriate to both junior high and high school
students and adults—the range of students for which these
materials are intended.

Examples:

```
┌─────────────────┐  ┌─────────────────┐  ┌─────────────────┐
│ VALUE           │  │ VALUE           │  │ VALUE           │
│ Honesty         │  │ Peace           │  │ Property        │
│ Communication   │  │ Absence of      │  │ Ownership and   │
│                 │  │ conflict or     │  │ control of land │
│                 │  │ tension         │  │ or goods        │
└─────────────────┘  └─────────────────┘  └─────────────────┘
```

It may be best, especially with more difficult concepts such as
love or justice, to leave the central box empty of anything but
the name of the concept itself. Brief definitions or explanations
for concepts like these may run the risk of seeming inadequate
or distorted.

```
┌────────────┐
│ EXAMPLES   │
└────────────┘
```

The box immediately above the central one can be used to cite
instances in which the particular value under discussion
was—or is—present. These can include cases discussed
previously during Debate and Rational Strategy exercises, in
addition to any ideas that developed from previous Awareness
Strategy activities. It should also include new examples.

      Thinking up new examples or instances is, in a sense,
the ultimate proof that the skill of identifying value questions

has been achieved. It also indicates to the teacher how close students are to understanding the basic concept at hand. Brainstorming techniques can be used to generate new examples (see page 45).

A few "facilitating" or "lead" questions like the following may prove helpful:

- What would be another case of [the value]?
- In what situations is [the value] important?
- What people might be most interested in or likely to show [the value]?
- Who is the most [adjectival form of the value; "honesty" would become "honest," and so on] person you know? How does he or she show this quality? What kinds of things has he or she done in the past to show it?

Other aspects of the value may be mentioned, and they can be saved for later on.

The contents of the boxes surrounding the concept name will probably overlap considerably, but there's no harm in this. If the same idea or term appears in more than one box, it only shows that it's related in more than one way to the value under discussion. Students will be more likely to consider a value from a different point of view if it appears in more than one place in the model; thus, what may first appear to be confusing can become beneficial.

BENEFITS

The box to the upper right of the central one should contain a list of the benefits that might come from upholding the value. It will help to think of these benefits in very concrete terms (see the examples below). One of the most common mistakes that moral education teachers make is to approach a problem from an abstract level while their students are thinking primarily in concrete terms. The case study strategies force the discussion of moral issues into concrete terms, and it's generally best to keep it there by touching base with concrete realities as often as possible even while teaching value concepts. Benefits, or possible benefits, can therefore be stated in concrete terms.

After all, if we're going to talk to students about upholding values, we ought to be able to tell them what these values are good for!

Facilitating questions like the following will be helpful here, too:

- What is [the value] good for?
- What might happen to you if you were [adjectival form of value]? What kinds of things would you do?
- What would it be like to be [adjectival form of value]? What kinds of things would you do?
- What do other people have who are [adjectival form of value]?
- What benefit does society get from [the value]? How is it good for people?

Examples:

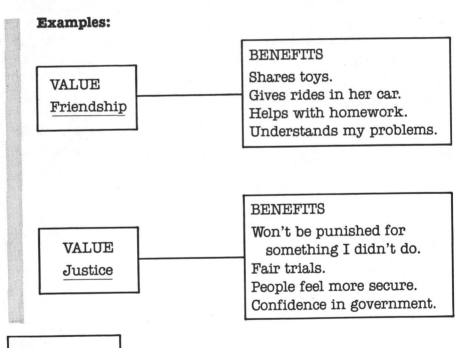

| VALUE
Friendship | BENEFITS
Shares toys.
Gives rides in her car.
Helps with homework.
Understands my problems. |

| VALUE
Justice | BENEFITS
Won't be punished for something I didn't do.
Fair trials.
People feel more secure.
Confidence in government. |

LIMITATIONS

Limitations are the opposite of benefits. Upholding one value when another value is at stake can be too much of a good thing and cause its own set of problems. Values have their limits, and exercising any particular value in too absolute a manner brings it into conflict with other equally strong or stronger values.

This may result in societal disapproval, since society defines the bounds of certain actions by means of social pressures. At times, the exercise of a certain value may actually be illegal.

The box in the lower right of the model provides space for these considerations. Facilitating questions might include:
- How can [the value] get you into trouble?
- What might happen if you were too [adjectival form of value]?
- Is [the value] always a good thing? (Consider, for example, "peace at any price.")
- How do people express their disapproval of [the value]?
- Are there any laws which limit [the value]?

Examples:

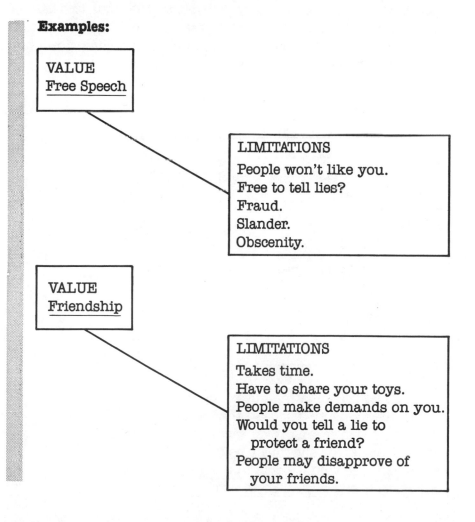

VALUE
Free Speech

LIMITATIONS
People won't like you.
Free to tell lies?
Fraud.
Slander.
Obscenity.

VALUE
Friendship

LIMITATIONS
Takes time.
Have to share your toys.
People make demands on you.
Would you tell a lie to
    protect a friend?
People may disapprove of
    your friends.

SIMILAR VALUES

Values are often related in that they both support and oppose one another. The remaining areas of the value concept model (the two boxes to the left) explore these relationships.

In the Similar Values box, then, one can list not only synonyms (such as bravery for courage, or fairness for justice) but also values which seem to be positively correlated with the concept under discussion. For example, does an increase or decrease in one generally bring about a corresponding increase or decrease in the other? The similarities need not be too close, and in many cases the relationships may be ambiguous; that is, the same two values may support each other in some cases and conflict in others. No definite system of such relationships can be described, since concepts aren't that systematic.

Examples:

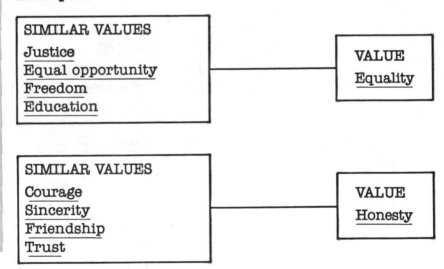

Useful facilitating questions include:
- What words might mean the same thing as [the value]?
- If a person is [adjectival form of value], what are some other things that he or she might be?
- When [the value] exists in a certain circumstance or among a certain group of people, what else would you expect to find?

In considering similar values, it's also helpful to explore priorities, although this is usually a question of individual preferences and thus more closely relates to the moral education objectives of the Awareness Strategy. Some questions to implement prioritizing include:

- Which is more important for society, [the value], or [the similar value]?
- Would you rather be [adjectival form of value], or [adjectival form of the similar value]?
- Which value was most important to [some person or group of people, such as the Puritans or the American Indians]?

CONFLICTING VALUES

Any case that poses a genuine moral problem is bound to produce a conflict of values. In looking for values which oppose the one under consideration, it will be helpful to recall cases considered in the past. If Identification and Summary Charts (see pages 59 and 62) have been kept, the Values Denied column will be a useful resource.

Honesty, for example, is generally a quality of good friendship, and the two can be considered to be similar or at least correlated. At times, though, one may lose friends by being "too honest." In other words, similar values can sometimes come into conflict. When honesty is being considered, then, friendship might be placed in both the Similar and Conflicting Values boxes. This apparent contradiction can lead students to consider the complex relationships between the two values of friendship and honesty.

Facilitating questions for identifying conflicting values might include:

- What's the opposite of [the value]?
- If [the value] weren't present, what other value might be? (Kindness instead of justice, for example.)
- If someone weren't [adjectival form of value], what else might he or she be that could also be considered good? (Tactful instead of honest, for example.)
- In [a case discussed earlier], why did some people say that [the value] was not very important?

Examples:

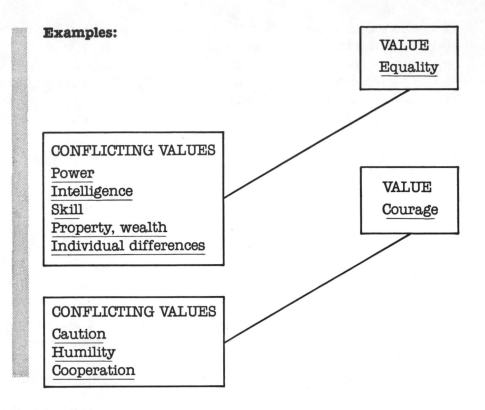

VALUE
Equality

CONFLICTING VALUES
Power
Intelligence
Skill
Property, wealth
Individual differences

VALUE
Courage

CONFLICTING VALUES
Caution
Humility
Cooperation

Classroom Procedures for Constructing Value Concept Models

A value concept model can, of course, be constructed on the chalkboard, and the teacher can work with the whole class to fill in the boxes. While this would certainly be a good way to introduce concept models, it's much more effective if the model chart (page 63) is duplicated as a worksheet for small-group discussions. This approach normally allows more students to participate in completing the model. The worksheets can also be used individually, but the interplay of ideas and suggestions combined with the experience of trying to use a concept in talking with other people seems to be the best of all possible atmospheres for developing or understanding concepts.

Students who work together in small groups often find their attention drawn to new aspects of the concept in question. It should be emphasized that students don't have to follow any particular order of steps when filling in the boxes; the considerations which surround a concept are often too interrelated and overlapping to allow this to happen.

Students in small groups can be supplied with the facilitating questions ahead of time or during their discussions, but once they have the idea of the basic outline of the model, it's best to omit this direct help. Otherwise, the task of constructing the model may become a simple matter of answering the questions. The teacher should always have the questions in mind, however, and be willing to help the various small groups by using the questions to direct their thinking into certain areas.

The following chart of facilitating questions may be helpful to the teacher and, if it seems like a good idea to duplicate it for them, to the students as well.

Value Concepts vs. Moral Concepts: From the Concrete to the Abstract

The Concept Strategy as explained here concentrates primarily on the concepts of social values and may seem to neglect the other set of concepts mentioned in the first section of this chapter—such as conscience, rights, and duties. These latter concepts require a slightly different teaching approach because they belong to a higher level of abstraction. Instead of referring to ideal social situations, they refer to aspects of our moral thought. It's generally a good idea to refer to the more abstract concepts as "moral concepts" while referring to the more concrete ones as "value concepts."

The reason for this Handbook's focus on value concepts is very simple: Young people use moral concepts less frequently than value concepts in the course of their normal conversation. This is not to say, of course, that we can't teach moral concepts to students, but it does put such concepts at the top of any list of moral education objectives in terms of their degree of difficulty. We might wish, for example, that young people would learn how to discuss the relationship of rights to duties, but we should never forget that the thinking of a great many young people is still at a very concrete level, and this sort of discussion may be difficult if not impossible for them. The

CONCEPT STRATEGY—FACILITATING QUESTIONS

EXAMPLES (Cases)

What would be another case of _____?

In what situations is _____ important?

What people might be most interested in or likely to show _____?

Who is the most _____ person you know?

SIMILAR VALUES

What words might mean the same thing as _____?

If a person is _____, what are some other things that he or she might be?

When _____ exists in a certain circumstance or among a certain group of people, what else would you expect to find?

VALUE

CONFLICTING VALUES

What's the opposite of _____?

If _____ weren't present, what other value might be?

If someone weren't _____, what else might he or she be that could also be considered good?

In _____ (a case discussed earlier), why did some people say that _____ was not very important?

(Cases)

How does he or she show this quality?

What does he or she do to show it?

What kinds of things has he or she done in the past to show it?

Name

Definition or explanation

BENEFITS

What is _____ good for?

What might happen to you if you were _____?

What would it be like to be _____?

What kinds of things would you do?

What do other people have who are _____?

What benefit does society get from _____?

How is it good for people?

LIMITATIONS

How can _____ get you into trouble?

What might happen if you were too _____?

Is _____ always a good thing?

How do people express their disapproval of _____?

Are there any laws which limit _____?

student who's able to develop concepts of social values has made a significant advance in moral growth. Value concepts are sufficiently challenging to the imagination that no student (or teacher) should feel unchallenged or disappointed if attention doesn't shift to the more abstract moral concepts.

There's also a pedagogical difficulty in presenting students whose thinking is still largely concrete with concepts they're not at all prepared to assimilate. This is especially important in the area of moral education. Decision-making is a practical activity which everyone must learn to do for himself or herself on his or her own level; to feel that there are "all those sophisticated moral concepts," as one teacher put it, can be depressing and undermine one's self-confidence. In physics or mathematics, for example, a student isn't expected to grasp theories before learning the basics. Similarly, no student of moral education should be expected to comprehend the most abstract concepts without first learning about society's expectations and norms.

The analogy ends here, however. While the student of mathematics or physics is frequently willing to defer to higher authorities for the correct answer to a problem without completely understanding the answer or how it was arrived at, no such authority exists in moral education. No one person can have all the "right" moral answers. To create the presumption, therefore, that there are moral experts who understand "all those sophisticated moral concepts" is to give a false impression of what morality is. This approach plays into the myth of expertise which so often dominates our thinking—and can lead straight into the dangers of indoctrination.

From an educational perspective, then, it isn't always best to "advance" to the discussion or teaching of abstract moral concepts. As teachers, we ourselves might develop concepts like these to a high level and take pride in our sophisticated understanding of them, but we should also beware of what might be termed the "professor's presumption," that is, the feeling that the latest and most sophisticated information we've learned, or the most recent perspective we've attained, is the one that desperately needs to be taught even in elementary schools. There is, of course, a proper time to move to the level of more abstract moral concepts, but that time doesn't arrive during high school for very many students. Presenting concepts or dwelling too long at a level far above the operative decision-making capabilities of students simply turns them off.

Despite these reservations, there is a time and a place for dealing with these higher concepts, and the moral educator ought to be prepared to do it. Unlike concepts of social values, moral concepts seem to have little in common with one another; they're related but often very independent notions. It's difficult, therefore, to develop a teaching model which can be used with all of these different concepts. It may be best to prepare a separate teaching model for each; fortunately, there aren't a great many of them that come up in common moral discussions. Only some very general approaches will be mentioned here.

Along these lines, activities for developing moral concepts might include:

- Listing instances.
  What are the duties of parents?
  What would you consider to be universal
  human rights?
- Listing counter-examples.
  Does everyone have a right to own an
  automobile? An airplane? To have a job?
  Is it a duty to vote?
- Discussing problem instances.
  Do people have a right to medical care?
  To a minimum income?
  Is a person responsible if he or she doesn't
  know the consequences of a specific
  action before taking it?
- Comparing theories.
  Is conscience the voice of God, or the voice of society?
  Where do rights and duties come from?
- Attempting definitions.
  Should the right to vote include the right
  to elect all government officials
  (including Supreme Court justices,
  for example), or only some?
  Should freedom of the press include the right
  for one newspaper to advertise against
  its competitors?

- Analyzing texts or statements.
  List the rights mentioned in the Declaration
  of Independence.
  "If someone has a right, then someone
  else has a duty." What does this
  statement mean? Is it always true?

It must be emphasized again that any concept, no matter how simple it may appear to be, is too broad and vague and bears too wide a range of interpretations to be captured by a single, memorizable definition. Understanding is developed through use, which gradually leads to familiarity. Using and analyzing a concept, not memorizing a definition or explanation, is what builds understanding of that concept.

To some people, of course, moral thinking is almost entirely a matter of learning to use these concepts, and there is much to be said for the current efforts of philosophers to reinstate abstract thinking in the curriculum. The approach taken in this Handbook is not intended to minimize the importance of educational efforts of this sort; much more experimentation is needed in this area. For the present, however, we can only hope that this brief outline of starter questions and ideas will help.

Chapter 6:
The Game Strategy:
When Playing Becomes
Learning

The fifth strategy for moral education, like the Awareness Strategy (see pages 23-32), is a general type of learning activity rather than a single model or teaching plan.

Teachers have used simulation games and role play with great success for many years now; unfortunately, the number of teachers who use these techniques is still relatively small, and the techniques themselves are often treated as "extra" or "supplementary" materials rather than primary teaching strategies. The myth still persists that education is work and that no one can learn anything through play.

The aims and objectives of moral education are so close to the kinds of learning experiences that students have during games and role play, though, that there can be little doubt about the appropriateness of these strategies. First, and most obviously, games and simulations put the student into the role of a participant who's asked to make certain decisions and act on them. Game and role-play strategies are always student-centered and focus on decisions. The whole of a game or role play thus constitutes direct experience in decision-making, and experience itself serves a definite purpose in terms of the objectives of moral education.

Secondly, the student who's placed in a role, whether in a simulation game or a role play, is apt to become aware—empathetically, we would hope—of others' feelings and perspectives. This is especially likely when the role in which a student is placed requires him or her to make a decision and actually experience the dilemma of being pulled in two directions at once by competing values.

A third aspect of games and role play is that they require students to attempt to foresee the consequences of their decisions. This, of course, is another major objective of moral education. In structured games, the possible courses of action are limited, and students soon become aware that the different courses available to them lead to different consequences. In Monopoly, for example—from which young people often learn more about the economic system than they do from social studies books—a player presented with the opportunity to buy a piece of property soon realizes that while his or her finances may be somewhat depleted, this purchase will give him or her something to bargain with, trade, or sell at a profit later on in the game. As a young person comes to realize the consequences of choices like these, he or she becomes a better decision-maker. In less structured games, and in role play, students are required to imagine and play out their own alternatives, thus exercising the imaginative skills important to decision-making as well.

Finally, games, simulations, and role play sometimes contribute to the social interaction objectives of moral education better than any other strategy can. In awareness activities, and in small group work, cooperation between students is certainly required; in games and role play, students must not only work together but must also face the whole range of other people's motives (whether cooperative or competitive) and attempt to predict their decisions. Games, simulations, and role play thus put decision-making into the context of real life to a degree unmatched by other strategies.

Playing Games in the Classroom

Since games don't follow any single model or pattern, it's impossible to describe them in general terms. An example may be the best way of illustrating many of the characteristics of this technique.

The game Democracy, written by James Coleman,* is a simulation well suited to moral education objectives in political science or American studies courses. Participants are cast in the roles of "legislators" who must vote for or against certain bills. They are also given some definite instructions from their

*James S. Coleman and Academic Games Associates, Inc., Democracy. New York: Western Publishing Co., 1969.

constituencies as to what legislation they should favor and what they should attempt to defeat. The instructions from the constituencies, which are distributed at random, also indicate the scores legislators will receive if their particular special-interest bills are passed or defeated. As students play to increase their scores, they become aware of the pressures politicians are often under and begin to realize some of the "deals" they must make among themselves.

In the second round of the Democracy game, another factor is added to the decision-making process: The legislators must consider their own feelings about the bills in question. Rather than merely attempting to fulfill the desires of their constituencies, then, the participants must respond to the pressure of attempting to be true to their own convictions as well. In short, the game focuses on the decisions that must be made, the pressures legislators feel (the teacher can use a value identification strategy to analyze them as value concepts), and the interaction of competition, cooperation, and compromise.

Democracy is a good game for moral education; others are less so. In reviewing and constructing games (many are now available commercially), moral education teachers—or teachers in other subjects who adopt moral education objectives—will want to keep these questions in mind:
• Does the game really put students in the role of decision-makers? (Some games are mere simulation exercises in which all decisions are predetermined.)
• Is there a range of alternatives for which students will have to calculate consequences?
• Does the game require interaction (competition or cooperation) among participants? (In some games, the interaction is limited to the individual participant and the game itself.)

A few games developed at the Moral Education Project of the College of Steubenville/Bethany College are included in the materials in Part III. Teachers who are unfamiliar with educational games may want to look these over and read through a few of the games before attempting to use any with a class. (It doesn't really matter what field of study these games are from, since the techniques of most of them are similar.) Although no overall teaching plan can be given for facilitating games in the classroom, the following pointers should prove helpful:

1. A teacher should never attempt to "control" a class in usual fashion during a game or simulation. Different students will probably be doing different things at the same time, and the teacher won't be able to govern or even observe all of them at once. The game itself and its structure are the true "controls." Many teachers are uneasy about this at first, and may need to learn to trust both the game plan and the students.

2. After a game has been introduced and explained, it will take a little time before it can get going properly. Students won't quite know what they're supposed to do at first and may need to figure out their roles by discussing the matter among themselves. A teacher needs to have the patience to allow this process enough time to work itself out. The same sort of thing occurs whenever one attempts to teach a new board or parlor game to children; it just takes a while for new players to comprehend all the rules.

3. Students may begin by doing all the wrong things, or may not at first follow the order of the game exactly. The teacher should let them figure it out; too much direction will only give students the feeling that they're supposed to play the game to satisfy the teacher rather than themselves.

4. After students have had a chance to become familiar with a game, or if a game doesn't seem to work out exactly as it should, many teachers choose to change the rules or legislate new ones. Sometimes, situations arise in the middle of a game for which there are no rules; sometimes, the teacher finds that a new rule will move the focus of interaction to a more desirable area. Rules aren't sacred; teachers who use games on a regular basis often say that they run them "in their own way."

5. Finally, the follow-up of a game is almost as important as the game itself. Students should be asked to compare experiences, be questioned about their intentions and actions during a game, and be instructed to reflect on their feelings and opinions. Different students will often learn different things during a game or simulation, but this doesn't mean that they can't be asked to analyze their experiences.

Moving into Role Play

In some respects, role play can be more difficult than simulations or games for both students and teachers. By nature, it involves fewer rules and requires more creativity. It's well worth it, though, since the skills necessary for effective role play are also necessary for effective decision-making. As is the case with stimulating class discussions, the teacher should make it clear that there are some things to be learned and should be willing to take time with the class to teach and learn them. With some effort, then, role play can work well, and both students and teachers will reap the educational benefits. Only when young people are expected to perform in ways they don't understand, or to use skills they haven't developed, are they likely to rebel and refuse to cooperate.

Role play can be used simply to present a case problem for discussion, or it can serve as an elaborate method of actually working through problems. A special advantage of role play is that when someone takes a certain action—for example, by making a decision or a specific statement—observers can always be asked to say how they would have done it. Since we're all better at hindsight than at foresight, and generally profit by realizing later what we should have said or done earlier, role play gives everyone the chance to gain by someone else's experience.

Setting the Scene

For the purpose of moral education, the role play situation will generally be one where there's a decision to be made. This means that when people are given roles to play, someone will need to be given a fairly specific question to ask or problem to resolve.

> **Examples:** [The following are the teacher's instructions to the class.]
>
> 1. You're a teacher, and you've caught Johnny, one of your students, stealing pencils. You've aready spoken to him about it, but now you have to decide whether or not to call his parents. This is his third offense, and you've warned him twice before.

2. You're a real estate agent, and you're trying to sell a house to Mr. and Mrs. Jones. You can tell them anything you want to about the house, but you must decide whether or not to tell them that the well has gone dry. If they buy the house, they'll have to have a new well drilled at a cost of $2,000.

A role should always be specific enough to give students something to work with—perhaps even something definite to say—but open enough to allow them to play it themselves in their own ways. At first, when working with students who are inexperienced in role play, it might be best to give them a fairly complete description of each role; later on, they'll be better equipped to make of a role whatever they wish.

It's important to describe a role-play situation imaginatively to the whole class, and moving the furniture around in a room to set the stage can help enormously. Often, it's a good idea to begin describing the situation before assigning roles. If students can get an idea of the scene and characters ahead of time, they'll be more likely to volunteer. They may even volunteer each other if they have some idea of who the "best actors" in the class are. At any rate, taking some time to describe the situation gives students a chance to imagine what they might say. Leaving time for students to prepare their parts is crucial to an effective role play. True, the role play should be somewhat spontaneous—but it should never be rushed.

Interaction

A role play which becomes a subject for class discussion doesn't have to be a long, drawn-out affair. Usually, a scene should last no more than four or five minutes (the preparation will take longer than the role play itself). Students should be told this ahead of time; if they know that they're expected to give only a short performance, they'll worry less about being "in the spotlight" with nothing to say. It does, however, normally take a minute or two to get the action going, even after the teacher has given the word to start, and the teacher can lessen the pressure of a role play by showing or saying that there's no problem if actors cause minor delays while thinking of what they want to say.

Furthermore—although this is more often necessary in an extended role play than a brief one—there's no harm in coaching students by giving them a new idea or way to bring out what they want to say. In some classes, this teacher interference is resented, or seems to break up the scene, but in other classes (especially those with slower students) it seems welcome, and the play goes on with little or no recognition of the outside help.

It's also possible for the teacher to play one of the roles. Students seem to like the idea of the teacher playing along with them, and sometimes a role may be a little too subtle or complex for students to grasp.

Follow-up Analysis

Class discussion of a role play usually takes longer than the scene itself and can easily lead to replaying the scene with new lines. It's helpful to let the major characters talk about how they felt while playing the parts; in addition to encouraging these and other immediate reactions to a role play or an evaluation, a number of general questions like the following can be useful:

- Why did _____ say what he or she did?
- How do you think [another character in the role play] felt when [the first character] said that?
- What else might [the first character] have said, and how would [the second character] have felt then?
- What was _____'s problem?
- What if he or she had decided to do the opposite [for example, to call the boy's parents]?
- Does anyone want to try the scene from that viewpoint and see if it would come out differently?

This last question can lead either to a replay or to an entirely new scene, since the teacher can take the opportunity to change the situation slightly by adding new facts or new considerations which the original actors neglected.

Group Decisions

One general type of role play that's especially effective with students who are unfamiliar with the technique is the situation in which a group of people (such as a board, committee, council, or whatever) has to make a specific decision. The group can delegate a chairperson whose task (explained ahead of time in a role description) is to see to it that the group does come to a definite decision. The group itself can be composed of from six to eight students. As a role play for beginners, this type of scene has the advantage of putting no one in particular on the spot; any member of the group can say something, but no one has to.

Dr. Robert C. Hawley has suggested another technique for reducing the pressure to perform which students sometimes feel during role plays. In the "Open Chair" method, the chair of the person who is the focus of attention in the role play is left empty, and three students are assigned to play that one part jointly by standing behind the open chair. Any of the three can speak for the character, but again, no one has to; there's no pressure to go it alone.*

Another general type of role play that can be used in the midst of a group discussion, especially after students are somewhat familiar with the technique, is the quick one of "What would you say?" When a problem arises in which what one person says to another would make a difference to the situation, any student or number of students in turn can be asked to respond immediately "in character" to one of the actors in the role play.

Examples: [These have been used during actual class discussion of case problems; the following are the teacher's instructions to the students.]

1. John, if you were the doctor and Jim here were your patient, how would you tell him that his disease was incurable? Go ahead, tell him; then we'll give someone else a chance.

*For a good discussion of role-play techniques with reference to moral education objectives, see Robert C. Hawley, Value Exploration Through Role Play. New York: Hart Publishing Co., 1975.

2. Mary, if Keith here were your little boy and had just asked you if it's true that his father was in jail once for forging checks, what would you tell him? (It is true, but it happened a long time ago.) Don't tell me [the teacher]; speak directly to Keith here, and then we'll see how he feels about it. Let's imagine that Keith is about six years old.

3. Fred, imagine that you've just backed your car out of your driveway and into Tom's car. Tom is your neighbor, and you have to tell him about it. Here's Tom next to you; he's just answered his door. Go ahead. How would you tell him?

Many times during class discussions, a role play can take the place of a direct question or answer. Role play slows the discussion down a little, but in ways which often help students to focus on exactly what's being said. This can make almost any discussion much more "real," and a topic can get carried a lot further than it would be otherwise. The opportunities are there if teachers have the techniques at hand and are willing to use them.

Part III:
Materials for the Moral Education Classroom

Chapter 7:
Justice:
A Social Studies Unit

The concept of justice is complex; it often has completely different meanings in different situations and realms of discourse. For example, legal justice and moral justice aren't always the same thing; often, they seem to conflict with one another. One common meaning of the concept is that of a punishment—such as a legal punishment, or one imposed by a parent, teacher, or superior; another encompasses the notion of fairness when something, such as a reward, is being distributed. These two meanings differ greatly, but a relationship between them does exist and can be useful in the moral education classroom.

The first meaning is actually related to the second historically. In the past, punishment was often thought of as retribution or fair repayment to society or to a victim. This unit centers on the notion of justice as equity or fairness (distributive justice) and raises questions of legal punishment only as they concern fair distribution. The question of distributive justice ought not to be separated from the problem of punishment, however, especially when teaching young people, since young people are often very much concerned about the justice of the rules and penalties which directly affect their lives.

In the authoritarian or legalistic perspective characteristic of the earlier stages of moral development, equity is viewed primarily in the context of punishment. The two meanings of the term are thus more closely related in the minds of young people than they are in the minds of adults; the question of punishment, then, will be used here to introduce the more general issue of fairness.

The Awareness Strategy

Awareness activities for this unit focus students' attention on their feelings about fair and unfair treatment, which they're often inclined to see as questions of punishment and of school or family rules. The teacher may find it helpful to refer to the description of the Awareness Strategy found on pages 23-32.

"Memories": Drawing from the Past

The Memories activity simply asks students to recall personal experiences and feelings which they perceive as involving fairness, equality, rewards, and punishment. It's intended to introduce the topic of justice by identifying some of people's past experiences as problems of justice or injustice.

It's helpful when establishing the atmosphere of this activity if the teacher first gives an indication of the types of experiences that may be recounted by telling one of his or her own. This will make the students more comfortable about relating their own stories.

The format of the exercise can vary, of course, according to the interaction pattern that works best in the particular class. The following Memory questions are of the general type that will help students to focus on feelings of fairness and injustice.

- Try to remember a time when someone was unfair to you. It might, for example, be a time when that person gave more of something to someone else than to you. It doesn't matter if you've changed your mind about the event since then; we're looking for situations when at that time you felt that someone was being unfair to you. It also doesn't matter if the person didn't mean to be unfair. Take a minute or two to think about it. It could have been a teacher, a brother or sister, a police officer, a friend, or anyone at all.

The materials in this unit are presented sequentially, beginning with awareness activities which introduce the topic and ending with conceptual abstractions. They can be used in any order, however, according to the teacher's approach or the demands of the course in which they are included.

- Can you remember a time when someone was unfair to someone else and gave you more of something than you should have received? Or, even if it wasn't quite unfair, a time when someone else felt that he or she was being treated unfairly because he or she thought that you had received more of something?
- Were you ever accused of doing something you hadn't really done? Try to recall a time when someone—a teacher or a parent, for example—thought that you'd done something you hadn't done. How did you feel? And what did you do?
- Was anyone else ever accused of doing something that you'd done? And did you admit to doing it? Or was there ever a time when you did something and didn't get caught?
- Can you think of a time when you were really angry with someone, so angry that you wanted to get back at that person by doing something that would hurt him or her? Why were you angry? Were you ever angry with anyone when you shouldn't have been? For example, what about a time when someone hurt you without meaning to, when it was just an accident?

Some of these Memory questions can lead to role plays of social situations. (See, for example, the "What would you say?" role play on page 84.) These might include:
- Talking with someone who's angry and won't listen.
- Trying to get two people back together again after a misunderstanding.
- Apologizing to someone for something you've done to him or her.
- Forgiving someone for something he or she has done to you.

Some of the memories which students come up with may not be personal experiences which have been resolved in the past, but real problems which still bother them. The students expressing them may feel very resentful or have other emotions which the teacher may not want to encourage them to express fully in the public atmosphere of a classroom. It often happens that a student is quite willing to discuss a rather personal matter and may only later be embarrassed about having revealed too much. Compositions sometimes contain personal confessions, as most teachers have discovered to their great surprise at one time or another, but compositions aren't public statements, and teachers are able to deal with these instances personally and privately. A class discussion is neither the time nor the place to deal with students' deeper feelings or personal problems. Teachers can, however, find a level of discussion which is very personal without going too far or carrying out group psychotherapy in the classroom. Students have a right to privacy, just as adults do, and sometimes they're too careless about protecting this right and later regret it. Teachers who are sensitive to this difficulty should be able to avoid these instances.

"Opinions on Punishment"

A second Awareness Activity related to the concept of justice asks students to give their opinions on punishment. The punishment discussed can be either legal (that is, administered by a court), institutional (by a school), or parental. This activity should draw attention to differences of opinion about punishment; these will, in a sense, be differences of judgment about what types of punishment are or aren't fair. These judgments will also reflect students' underlying feelings about whether punishment itself is a worthwhile instrument of educational, social, or family control.

The worksheet on pages 94-95 should be filled out individually. Students should be given ample time to complete it to their satisfaction.

Since punishment is for the most part a social rather than an individual decision, however, compromise and cooperation are also appropriate to this activity. A second step, therefore, can be that of small-group discussions—groups can contain from three to four students—with each group being instructed to agree upon the punishment in each case. A final class discussion can include voting on the punishments proposed by the small groups where differences of opinion exist.

The range of opinion can, of course, include no punishment at all if students don't see the particular action in question as a punishable offense.

The Debate Strategy

"Capital Punishment": Debating a Major Issue

Since questions of distributive justice typically involve more than two alternatives, thus requiring more complex approaches than the Debate Strategy normally encompasses, most of the important cases for this unit will be included in the Rational Strategy and Game Strategy sections. There are, however, a number of questions of fair punishment that can work well in a debate situation.

The major social issue of punishment today concerns the death penalty. This issue, however, is one on which students will probably already have established opinions. In some schools, or in some areas of the country, students may be unanimously in favor of or against capital punishment. The particular case chosen for the debate can be altered or a better one found if a reasonable division of opinion doesn't occur. In addition, a number of relevant questions can be introduced, such as:

- Has the death penalty decreased crime in other countries?
- Has crime increased in countries which no longer apply it?
- What's the relationship of the presence or absence of the death penalty to the number of specific offenses which occur, like unpremeditated murder or rape?

The issue can be a good one—if the teacher feels that sufficient class interest exists to warrant pursuing it—on which to arrange an extended debate after allowing students ample time for research. Students can be assigned to opposite sides of the debate if a division of opinion doesn't naturally occur. Since this is an important social issue which does have two sides, assigning students to defend one side or the other makes it a research assignment and doesn't necessitate their compromising their own opinions or feelings.

Three Cases: "Skyjackers," "Broken Windows," and "Ms. Robin"

The "Skyjackers" case which follows will probably raise most of the important considerations of capital punishment. The two other

OPINIONS ON PUNISHMENT WORKSHEET

This worksheet includes a list of eleven types of offenses for which people are often punished. What do <u>you</u> think is a fair punishment for each offense? Don't worry about what punishments are <u>usually</u> given by the courts, school, or parents. Think about what <u>you</u> would decide for each case.

      You may come up with as tough a penalty as you wish, or no punishment at all, as long as <u>you</u> think your decision is <u>fair</u>.

1. A five-year-old child takes cookies after his mother tells him that he isn't allowed to have any before dinner. _____

_____

_____

2. A high school student steals $10 from someone's locker. _____

_____

_____

3. A government employee sells government secrets to another country. _____

_____

4. A person drives a car while intoxicated (drunk). _____

_____

_____

5. A ten-year-old stays out until 8:00 P.M. when she was supposed to be home for dinner at 6:00 P.M. _____

_____

_____

94 ©Winston Press, Inc. Permission is given to reproduce this page for student use.

6. A doctor fails to report $10,000 of his income on his tax return.

_____

_____

7. A high school senior is caught in school with three marijuana cigarettes. _____

_____

8. A city official has received $8,000 from a contractor she had appointed to build a new road. _____

_____

9. A person commits armed robbery of a gas station. _____

_____

10. A state senator has received illegal campaign contributions.

_____

_____

11. A high school student takes his parents' car for the evening after they refuse him permission. _____

_____

©Winston Press, Inc. Permission is given to reproduce this page for student use.

cases which follow can be used according to the regular format of the Debate Strategy (see pages 33-42).

Other Debate Strategy cases in this Handbook which can be used in this unit include "Guard Duty," page 34; "Beauty Parlor," page 115; and "A Ghost from the Past," page 34.

SKYJACKERS

Three members of a terrorist group in your country recently hijacked an airplane and held the passengers captive, demanding the release of twelve other terrorists who are in prison for various crimes against the state. The government refused to give in to their demands, and when a military squad moved in to take the airliner, five passengers and two soldiers were killed. The three hijackers were captured and convicted on four charges, including murder of the passengers and soldiers.

The judge has told the jury that he will impose the death penalty, since terrorism is an increasing danger in the country. He can only do so if the jury recommends it, however. Keeping the three in prison, the judge has said, will only tempt other terrorists to kidnap more innocent victims in order to gain their release.

If you were a jury member, would you recommend the death penalty?

BROKEN WINDOWS

One evening, following a basketball game at your school, a near-riot developed in the parking lot, and some windows of an out-of-town school bus were broken. The school principal and the basketball coach have apologized to authorities at the other school, but they haven't been able to discover who was actually responsible for the damage. They have therefore decided to punish the whole student body: No local school buses will be allowed to transport students to out-of-town games unless the people who did the damage either turn themselves in or are found.

At a meeting of the student council, of which you are a member, one student says that she saw the incident and is willing to tell the principal who was responsible if the council votes that she should. She also says, however, that she feels that the situation in the parking lot was out of control and that everyone there was equally responsible. She believes that it might be more fair for the whole student body to accept the punishment.

The student council decides to vote on whether or not she should tell the principal what she saw.

How would you vote?

MS. ROBIN

Ms. Robin teaches history at City High. Due to an energy shortage, the Board of Education decided that the heat in the building would have to be turned down. It was then turned down to a level that many people found uncomfortable.

After a week of grumbling and complaints, a group of students submitted a petition to the principal asking her to turn up the heat. She responded that this was a School Board decision which she had to follow but that she would make an immediate attempt to get it changed.

Two days later, a group of about 100 students staged a protest (the total enrollment of City High is about 1,000) by staying out of classes and making as much noise as they could in the hallways. The principal reacted by suspending the protesters for four days and issuing a directive to teachers to give these students failing grades for the suspension period.

Ms. Robin uses a grading procedure based upon daily grades, and has planned an important examination for one of the suspension days. If she follows the principal's directive, four of her students who were suspended will end up with lower grades at the end of the semester than they would if they were allowed to attend class and take the exam.

Grade books and classroom procedure records must be turned in at the end of the term, so the principal could check on whether or not Ms. Robin complied with the directive.

Should Ms. Robin comply with the directive?

The Rational Strategy

Topics for Class Discussion

The cases which follow are suited to the Rational Strategy because more than one alternative is possible for each. The teacher may want to introduce the notion of justice as a <u>fair</u>

©Winston Press, Inc. Permission is given to reproduce this page for student use.

distribution of goods or a fair choice among people with a couple of quick examples or problems before going directly to the cases, however.

Justice is defined in dictionaries as equity, fairness, due reward, or equal distribution. In any situation where things (such as material goods, privileges, or responsibilities) are in limited supply and must be divided among people, the question of how to divide them can be raised. The following brief examples can be used as starters to show that there can be more than one way of calculating fairness.

- A family of two parents and two children, all with driver's licenses, has only one automobile. How can they decide who should get to use the car and when? [Equal time, parents have first choice, children have first choice, each person has it one day in order, whoever needs it gets it, etc.]
- A family has three children: a fourth grader, a fifth grader, and a seventh grader. Each child has always received the same allowance as the others. The oldest now says that she should get a little more since she's in junior high school. Is her request a fair one?
- During a family softball game, the mother suggests that the youngest child should be allowed four strikes instead of three since he's the smallest. Is this fair?
- Five people—two adults and three children—are shipwrecked on a desert island. They figure that they have enough food for five people for thirty days, but can't be sure when they'll be rescued. How should they divide the food? What would be the fairest way?

Three Cases: "The Sloppy Chef Layoff," "Oil Profits," and "Tax Reform"

The fact that there's more than one way to decide fairly in each of these examples leads directly to the search for alternatives which is important to an understanding of the following cases. The teacher may find it useful to consult the discussion of the Rational Strategy found on pages 43-50. (The "Oil Profits" case is a little more involved than the others; the teacher should plan enough time to work out the mathematics of the alternatives with students.)

Other Rational Strategy cases in this <u>Handbook</u> which can be used in this unit include "A Difficult Move," page 177; "Candy Store," page 119; and "Lost and Found," page 46.

THE SLOPPY CHEF LAYOFF

George Bates is the manager of a local branch of the Sloppy Chef hamburger chain. Although he's responsible for operating the restaurant, he's generally governed by company policies passed along to him by the regional director.

Business has been slow for six months, and the director has suggested that it may be necessary to cut back the number of employees at George's branch. George employs six men and five women, and all but two of the men have been with him since the restaurant first opened.

One day, George receives a letter from the head office stating that George must cut two employees from each of the two shifts. In addition, the letter states that it's normally company policy to lay off women before men because men are more likely to have family responsibilities and to remain with the company longer. Women, the letter continues, tend to leave the company at some point to raise families.

George wonders whether he should follow this policy. He knows it's discriminatory, and besides, three of the women he employs are his most competent workers. George realizes, however, that he isn't in a strong position to go against company policy and that doing so might jeopardize his future advancement opportunities.

What should George do?

OIL PROFITS

A very small country in the Middle East has suddenly "struck it rich": Huge oil deposits have been found in its territory. The government, which consists of an elected Prime Minister and a legislative body called the Council, owns all the oil and has successfully begun to export it.

The country is semi-socialist, which means that housing, transportation, medical services, education, and many other products and services are provided by the government. Even the farms have been nationalized, leaving relatively few independent business enterprises.

©Winston Press, Inc. Permission is given to reproduce this page for student use.

The population of the country is around 1,000 people. About 250 belong to the "wealthy class"; they are generally well educated business people, engineers (who run the oil industry), highly skilled workers, and professional people. The rest of the population—around 750 "poor" people—are uneducated and unskilled laborers. About 100 of the wealthy people are employed in the business and technical sections of the oil industry and in government; about 500 of the poor, including most children over twelve years old, work at low-paying jobs. Most wealthy people have savings in the banks, in addition to other financial resources.

The oil profits for the year, after government expenses, total $1,000,000. The government has decided to distribute these profits as wages among the people to use for food and clothing. Although this will give most people in the country more money than they've ever had before, the Secretary of Welfare has determined that the "poverty level" for food and clothing, below which people can't be adequately fed and clothed, is $1,200 per person per year.

The question before the Prime Minister and the Council is one of how to distribute the oil profits fairly.

How should they do it?

TAX REFORM

For many years now, there's been a lot of talk throughout the United States and in Congress about tax reform. People complain that taxes are too high, saying that the poor and middle-income groups pay the most while rich people and large corporations often pay little or nothing. Some say that the income tax itself isn't fair; others say it's more fair than sales taxes, property taxes, or inheritance taxes.

Think of as many different ways of taxing people as you can. Which one of these seems to you to be the most fair?

The Game Strategy

"Hospital Committee on Scarce Medical Resources"

The following game, "Hospital Committee on Scarce Medical Resources," is a case of distributive justice. It can be worked

 © Winston Press, Inc. Permission is given to reproduce this page for student use.

according to the Rational Strategy, but students usually find it more interesting if it's presented as a role play.

The scene can be enacted either by the class as a whole or by groups of from eight to ten students. Participants should be instructed to select a chairperson whose task it will be to see that the group arrives at a decision by majority vote. The teacher may wish to introduce the problem in his or her own way, but the account which follows on page 102 should suffice.

The three candidates each represent different sets of considerations. The housewife is important to her children; the steelworker is the breadwinner for his family; and the doctor is potentially most important for society as a whole. If students have further questions about the characters, the teacher can either make up answers (such as "The housewife's children are two, three, and five years old"; "The steelworker's wife has a heart condition and can't work"; "The doctor is in good health otherwise") or can simply say that further information isn't available. If the discussion seems to center primarily on one candidate (different classes will choose different candidates), some additional information, like the following, can be supplied to the class to help restore the balance:

• The steelworker has the most difficulty with the kidney machine treatment.
• One of the three [whoever seems to be the class favorite at the time] lost his or her kidney by taking an overdose of some poison when he or she tried to commit suicide.
• The housewife is the youngest of the three; perhaps she would benefit from the transplant longer than either of the other two.

The teacher may also want to add considerations about fair procedures, like the following:
• Perhaps the kidney donor should decide. Or, if the donor has died, then his or her family should have some say in the matter.
• Perhaps the committee should give each candidate an equal chance by asking them to draw straws.
• Perhaps the first candidate who applied should get it—first come, first served. [The teacher can say that the person who is considered least worthy by the class is the one who applied first.]

HOSPITAL COMMITTEE ON SCARCE MEDICAL RESOURCES

Many hospitals often have a problem in that there's a larger demand for certain resources than there are resources available. This problem can occur when there are human organs for transplant (such as eyes, kidneys, and hearts; sometimes even blood is scarce) or mechanical devices (such as respirators or kidney machines) which are so expensive that hospitals can't afford as many as are needed. When patients apply for these resources, a hospital must be careful to be as fair as possible when choosing among the patients. In some cases, hospitals have asked committees of non-medical people to act as independent juries for these types of decisions.

One case currently before the committee of a large metropolitan hospital concerns a kidney which will be available for transplant within the hour. Three people have recently applied for a kidney transplant; they are considered to be equally qualified from a purely medical point of view.

Mrs. X is a twenty-five-year-old housewife who has three small children. Her husband, a carpenter, has been working overtime to pay her medical expenses.

Mr. Y is a forty-year-old steelworker. He has two children who will finish high school this year and next and hope to go on to college. He lives some distance from the hospital, and it has been difficult for him to get enough time off from work for the kidney-machine treatments.

Dr. Z is a fifty-five-year-old neurosurgeon with two grown children. For the past five years, he has been developing a type of brain operation which may help to control epilepsy. He is the first person in the world to come up with this particular operation.

As a committee member, you are responsible for considering which of the three candidates should receive the donated kidney. You must work together with the other committee members to make the final decision.

Each candidate is currently using the kidney machine, which means that each has to travel to the hospital twice a week for treatments. The transplant isn't a life-or-death matter for any of the three—none will die if he or she isn't chosen—, but the treatments are a great inconvenience. If the transplant is successful, the person who receives the kidney will never have to use the machine again and can return to a more normal everyday life.

Which of the three should be chosen for the transplant—Mrs. X, Mr. Y, or Dr. Z?

"College Admissions"

The second game in this unit, a role play, deals with the problem of distributive justice on a more social level. The situation concerns the distribution of educational opportunities (another scarce resource) among people of different social and cultural backgrounds. It requires that the class be divided into three groups. The teacher should allow each group enough time to plan what it will say and do before the role play begins. The Admissions Board group should be told that while they can run the meeting in whatever way they choose, they must decide ahead of time how they will conduct the meeting—i.e., who will be allowed to speak and for how long. The two student groups should be instructed to plan their arguments carefully and to decide which of them will act as the representative speaker or speakers.

COLLEGE ADMISSIONS

City College is a community college in a small city. It is run by the state and supported by a combination of grants and alumni contributions. The student body consists of approximately 800 students.

This year, 400 students have applied for admission to the freshman class, but the Admissions Board can admit only a total of 200 students. The Admissions Board has called a meeting and invited representatives of two prominent student groups to speak before them.

One group consists of 200 students from predominantly upper-middle-class neighborhoods. Many of them have gotten good grades throughout high school and scored well on the college admissions tests. The schools in their neighborhoods have a generally good reputation, low student-faculty ratios, and excellent facilities. In addition, private tutors are made available on a regular basis, as are independent studies and other special courses.

©Winston Press, Inc. Permission is given to reproduce this page for student use. 103

The other group consists of 200 students from poorer sections of the city. Many of them are Black or of Spanish-American descent. The schools in their neighborhoods usually operate under less-than-desirable conditions—low budgets, high student-faculty ratios, and inadequate facilities. Thus, the students from these neighborhoods don't receive the educational benefits that the students from the upper-middle-class neighborhoods do, and this is often reflected in their grades and college admissions scores.

The first group feels that their high grades and scores should guarantee them places in the college. The second group feels that they've been disadvantaged and should receive consideration based on that fact.

During the meeting with the Admissions Board, each group will have the opportunity to state its case. Afterward, the Board will make a decision on how it will select the entering class for the following year.

The Concept Strategy

Topics for Class Discussion

If the teacher has been proceeding through this unit in order of the various strategies, the Concept Strategy outlined here will serve as a logical conclusion. Of the three steps in the Concept Strategy procedure—Explanation, Identification, and Modeling—the first has already been dealt with in detail, and the second shouldn't pose any problems. (The teacher may want to review the chapter on the Concept Strategy, pages 51-76.)

The cases chosen for this unit all serve to illustrate different aspects of the concept of justice, and it should be easy enough for students to look back through the cases and identify the different types of justice dealt with there. What may not be obvious to students is that different people look at the concept of justice in different ways, and that the value of justice can conflict with other values. In reviewing the cases previously studied, then, the teacher might want to point out examples of conflicting concepts of justice, of alternatives in which justice is a "value denied," and of other values which

104 © Winston Press, Inc. Permission is given to reproduce this page for student use.

seem to be highly correlated with justice. (The teacher might find it useful to review the Identification class procedures found on pages 57-62.)

Class discussions can focus on various understandings of the concept itself. To begin with, of course, there are the two concepts which were highlighted at the beginning of this unit—punishment and distribution. Discussion questions which will help to bring out these differences might include:

• Why does the word justice sometimes mean punishment and sometimes mean a fair share? [The teacher may or may not introduce the term distribution into this discussion.]
• How is fairness related to punishment?
• Is it ever fair to give different punishments to two people who have committed the same offense or crime?

Different understandings of the concept may also be viewed as different ways of calculating fairness in distributing certain things. The cases presented earlier in this unit will have generated alternative ways of calculating justice, and these may now be compared with one another. In general (but not strictly in all cases), three methods of calculating distributive justice can be discerned in each case:

1. Equality: giving each person an equal chance at something by some procedure such as drawing straws;

2. Need: giving more of something to someone who needs it more (such as the poor, minorities, handicapped or sick persons, or people with greater responsibilities); and

3. Merit: giving more of something to someone who deserves it more or who has earned it.

These three types of distributive justice can be brought out via a discussion of the previous cases and games, using the comparative chart which follows. Since a number of cases are available, it will be possible to discuss some of them (such as "The Sloppy Chef Layoff," page 99) in class, using the chart as a worksheet or a chalkboard model. Other cases, such as the "Hospital Committee on Scarce Medical Resources" (page 102) and "Tax Reform" (page 100), may be reserved for times when the chart can be used as an individual or group worksheet. The value of the chart is that it enables one to see the same type of distribution criteria applied to the various cases.

Sample Chart for Concepts of Justice Exercise:

	Case College Admissions
Equality	Lottery system.
Need	Give a certain number of admissions to minority students.
Merit	Admission by college entrance examination scores.

Modeling the Concept of Justice

The Concept Model techniques for justice will follow the standard plan introduced on pages 62-70. Again, the concept will entail both punishment and distribution; the model easily permits this, however, since the items on the modeling chart don't have to be related to one another. The teacher may want to refer to the Facilitating Questions chart on page 72.

The following is a sampling of the ideas that may be brought out in a class discussion of this nature. The examples are drawn from an actual discussion which took place in a high school class.

CONCEPTS OF JUSTICE WORKSHEET

	Case	Case	Case
Equality			
Need			
Merit			

©Winston Press, Inc. Permission is given to reproduce this page for student use. 107

Sample Concept Modeling Worksheet:

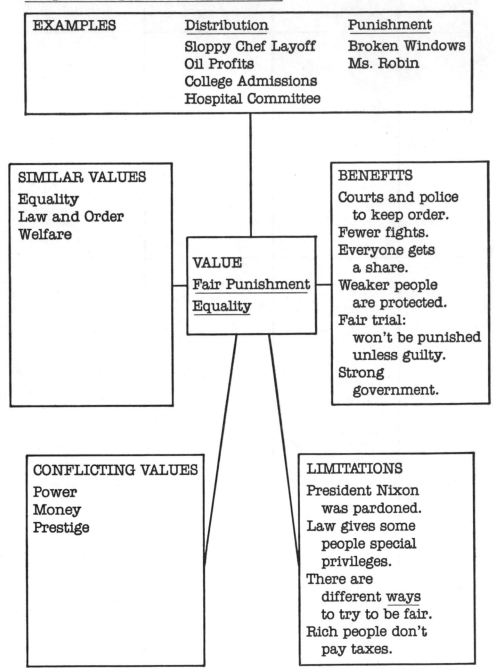

EXAMPLES	Distribution	Punishment
	Sloppy Chef Layoff	Broken Windows
	Oil Profits	Ms. Robin
	College Admissions	
	Hospital Committee	

SIMILAR VALUES
Equality
Law and Order
Welfare

VALUE
Fair Punishment
Equality

BENEFITS
Courts and police
  to keep order.
Fewer fights.
Everyone gets
  a share.
Weaker people
  are protected.
Fair trial:
  won't be punished
  unless guilty.
Strong
  government.

CONFLICTING VALUES
Power
Money
Prestige

LIMITATIONS
President Nixon
  was pardoned.
Law gives some
  people special
  privileges.
There are
  different ways
  to try to be fair.
Rich people don't
  pay taxes.

Chapter 8:
Property: A Business and Economics Unit

The Awareness Strategy

"Opinions on Business"

The worksheets which follow are three forms of a survey of "Opinions on Business." The initial purpose of these worksheets is to direct students' attention to their own feelings, opinions, and, in some cases, values. Instructions for their use are to "Circle the words which indicate your own agreement or disagreement with the statements"; it should be emphasized that there are no "right" or "wrong" answers.

After completing their worksheets, students should gather in small groups (of three or four each) to discuss their agreements and disagreements with the statements. They should be prepared to share their opinions and reasons for agreeing or disagreeing. Students may change their opinions during this discussion and should mark any changes on their papers.

Class discussion of some of the statements on which there seems to be a strong difference of opinion among students may be helpful. In addition, students can be given a writing assignment to defend their agreement or disagreement with different statements.

Forms II and III of the survey can be used later in the term; the materials in this unit are designed to be integrated into a regular business or economics course rather than used as a separate unit.

The teacher may want to consult the Awareness Strategy materials found on pages 23-32 prior to beginning this exercise.

The materials in this unit are presented sequentially, beginning with awareness activities which introduce the topic and ending with a simulation exercise. They can be used in any order, however, according to the teacher's approach or the demands of the course in which they are included.

OPINIONS ON BUSINESS: WORKSHEET I

Circle the words which indicate <u>your own</u> agreement or disagreement with each statement.

1. Collecting unemployment is as good a job as any other.

Strongly Agree   Agree   Disagree   Strongly Disagree

2. It's better to work for a large company than a small business.

Strongly Agree   Agree   Disagree   Strongly Disagree

3. All people are competitive.

Strongly Agree   Agree   Disagree   Strongly Disagree

4. The easiest job is the best.

Strongly Agree   Agree   Disagree   Strongly Disagree

5. No one likes work.

Strongly Agree   Agree   Disagree   Strongly Disagree

6. It's better to buy American products than foreign ones.

Strongly Agree   Agree   Disagree   Strongly Disagree

7. Friends should never get involved in business transactions with one another.

Strongly Agree   Agree   Disagree   Strongly Disagree

OPINIONS ON BUSINESS: WORKSHEET II

Circle the words which indicate <u>your own</u> agreement or disagreement with each statement.

1. You can believe advertisements.

Strongly Agree   Agree   Disagree   Strongly Disagree

2. Women make poor business people.

Strongly Agree   Agree   Disagree   Strongly Disagree

3. In business, it's OK to cheat a sucker.

Strongly Agree   Agree   Disagree   Strongly Disagree

4. Business is always cutthroat; competition is necessary.

Strongly Agree   Agree   Disagree   Strongly Disagree

5. Most people hate their jobs.

Strongly Agree   Agree   Disagree   Strongly Disagree

6. Government should never interfere with business.

Strongly Agree   Agree   Disagree   Strongly Disagree

7. Government should limit the size of corporations.

Strongly Agree   Agree   Disagree   Strongly Disagree

©Winston Press, Inc. Permission is given to reproduce this page for student use. 111

OPINIONS ON BUSINESS: WORKSHEET III

Circle the words which indicate your own agreement or disagreement with each statement.

1. Profit is the only reason for being in business.

Strongly Agree   Agree   Disagree   Strongly Disagree

2. Legislation is necessary to force industry to control pollution.

Strongly Agree   Agree   Disagree   Strongly Disagree

3. Advertising serves a useful purpose.

Strongly Agree   Agree   Disagree   Strongly Disagree

4. All people should have a right to work and to earn a living.

Strongly Agree   Agree   Disagree   Strongly Disagree

5. Major industries should all be owned by the government.

Strongly Agree   Agree   Disagree   Strongly Disagree

6. Business shouldn't be allowed to contribute to political campaigns.

Strongly Agree   Agree   Disagree   Strongly Disagree

7. When they're in business, people have to do things that they wouldn't otherwise do or approve of doing.

Strongly Agree   Agree   Disagree   Strongly Disagree

 © Winston Press, Inc. Permission is given to reproduce this page for student use.

"Hard Noses and Soft Noses"

Class Discussion

Using some of the questions from one of the "Opinions on Business" worksheets, develop a distinction between the characteristics of "Hard-Nosed Business People" and "Soft-Nosed Business People."

First, discuss this distinction with reference to the questions themselves. The students should be allowed to figure out for themselves what the distinction means.

Second, list the characteristics of each type in two columns on the chalkboard. Students may add any characteristics that seem to fit, but the teacher should try to direct attention to business-related characteristics.

Interview

Divide the class into pairs of students. Instruct them to interview each other and report to the class as to how each would rate his or her partner—as a Hard Nose or a Soft Nose. A five-point scale should illustrate the fact that the distinction is one of degree.

Soft Nose   1   2   3   4   5   Hard Nose

A demonstration interview—with the teacher interviewing a student, or vice versa—will show that there are good reasons to give someone a rating of 2 or 4 if he or she is generally Hard Nosed or Soft Nosed but occasionally has some reservations. The sense of the 2, 3, and 4 ratings should be made clear before the class interviews begin.

The teacher may also want to hold a demonstration interview and ask each student to write down independently what score he or she would give to the person being interviewed. Students should also record the reasons for their decisions. Class discussion of scoring disagreements will help students to get a feeling for the scale. Half numbers may be used if students want to make finer distinctions. Agreement on scoring isn't necessary as long as students get a good idea of how to conduct the evaluations.

After the interviews, students can be asked to write a paragraph giving the scores they assigned to their partners and the reasons for those scores. The reports can be read aloud and followed by class discussion. The interviewees should also have a chance to respond (by agreeing or disagreeing) to the score the interviewer assigned to them.

Values Identification
In class or small-group discussion, ask students to try to identify the Values Upheld and Values Denied for Hard-Nosed and Soft-Nosed business people respectively (see pages 59, 60). Values that can be assigned might include competitiveness, cooperativeness, self-reliance, security-mindedness, kindness, charity, politeness, honesty, and so on. It's also interesting to consider values which can't be easily assigned as upheld or denied by either Hard Noses or Soft Noses, such as reasonableness, responsibility, or courage. Finally, the problems of characterizing people too strictly and of attributing values to them too quickly should be discussed. Can we really say that one person is more honest, independent, or charitable than another?

The Debate Strategy

Five Cases: "Godfrey," "Beauty Parlor," "The Swedish Match King," "Breaking a Lease," and "Swenson Cable T.V."

The following cases are designed for use with the Debate Strategy, outlined on pages 33-42. Other Debate Strategy cases in this Handbook which can also be used in this unit include "Ms. Robin," page 97; "A New Job," page 175; and "Broken Windows," page 96.

GODFREY

Mary Murphy and Sharon Anderson are executive secretaries. They work for H.J. Godfrey, the new president of Jones Steel Products. Mr. Godfrey has recently replaced the last president, who was fired by the company's Board of Directors.

 © Winston Press, Inc. Permission is given to reproduce this page for student use.

The company has been losing money, and the directors have decided that a "get-tough policy" is necessary. Mr. Godfrey is a "no-nonsense" boss who puts pressure on all of the employees to do their jobs efficiently and quickly. Everyone knows that he's going to be firing some of the employees he feels the company can afford to do without.

The "get-tough policy" extends to everything. Recently, Mr. Godfrey told Mary and Sharon that he felt they weren't using their time very well, even though they always had their work completed on time. In particular, he said that he didn't approve of their "long" coffee-breaks. "People just gather around the coffee pot," he said, "and the whole company becomes a social organization. If you women want to spend all your time gabbing, you should stay home and be housewives. From now on, just take five minutes for a break."

This morning, Mr. Godfrey passed Sharon at the coffee maker and said, "That's more than five minutes. I hope you don't expect to be paid for it." A little while later, he handed her a memo to type. It was a note to the treasurer ordering him to cut Sharon's salary $50 a month; on the bottom he had scribbled "Wastes time!"

Sharon typed the memo, but she's been upset about it all day. She feels that Mr. Godfrey is being unfair. She hadn't taken much more than five minutes, although she hadn't timed it and couldn't really say that she'd taken less than five minutes, either. Both she and Mary had been taking shorter breaks, as Mr. Godfrey had told them to do, and had been getting all their work done on time as usual.

Not knowing what else to do, Sharon asks Mary to speak to Mr. Godfrey for her.

If you were Mary, would you do it?

BEAUTY PARLOR

As a manager of a neighborhood beauty parlor, you realize how important it is to keep your customers happy. Recently, because your business has been gaining a good reputation, customers have started to come in from different parts of the city rather than just from the local neighborhood. Some of the local people, however, don't like the new customers and have told you that they'll go elsewhere if you don't do

©Winston Press, Inc. Permission is given to reproduce this page for student use.

something to limit the number of Black and Puerto Rican women who are beginning to come.

"Just don't give them appointments," one woman has said. "You have enough business right here in the neighborhood anyway."

In fact, the great majority of your customers are women from your neighborhood, and you can hardly afford to lose their business. The beauty parlor has become a social center of sorts, and if your regular customers start to feel uncomfortable they'll probably move to one of your competitors. Once a few of them move, the rest will probably follow.

Would you take the woman's advice and refuse to serve the new customers?

THE SWEDISH MATCH KING

In 1933 Ivar Kreuger, a businessman known as the Swedish Match King, committed suicide in Paris.* He was the president of an international financial empire which was having severe problems. It had been built up through fraudulent practices, although this wasn't generally known at the time of Kreuger's death.

At the time of the suicide, an American stockbroker, C.E. Jones, was in Paris attending a business meeting. He happened to find out about the suicide and learned that Kreuger International stock would soon be worthless. Before the news got out to the general public, Jones telephoned his company in New York and told them to sell all of its Kreuger stock immediately. The company disposed of almost all of it—which did become worthless paper within the week.

At a hearing of the Senate Banking and Currency Committee, Jones was asked whether he felt justified in selling something he knew to be absolutely worthless to people who had no way of knowing this, even though it was apparently legal for him to do so.

Would you have done it?

*The facts of this case are taken from an article in the London Evening Standard, May 6, 1933.

 ©Winston Press, Inc. Permission is given to reproduce this page for student use.

BREAKING A LEASE

When the stock market crashed, Mr. Sarkis lost nearly all he had. He was living in an expensive apartment at the time and decided at once that he would have to move.

Mr. Sarkis asked his landlord to let him break his lease, but the landlord refused. He said that because of the depression he would never be able to rent the apartment to anyone else, and that he needed the money more than ever. Mr. Sarkis pleaded with the landlord to at least let him move into a cheaper apartment in the same building. Finally, the landlord agreed.

As soon as Mr. Sarkis moved, he claimed that the landlord had broken the original lease and refused to sign the new lease for the cheaper apartment. The following week, Mr. Sarkis moved out of the building.

Was what Mr. Sarkis did fair?

SWENSON CABLE T.V.

Nels Swenson has been the head of a small cable T.V. firm for six years. Since a considerable investment was needed to form this company, stock was sold on the local market.

Because of the nature of the industry, the company can operate in either of two phases: an "expansion" phase, during which, with considerable investment in new lines and equipment, the T.V. cable is brought into a new area; or a "retrenchment" phase, during which income is high from existing installations but little growth occurs. During expansion, the firm has to rent equipment for installing new lines and also employs nearly twice as many people as it does during retrenchment. Each of the two phases lasts about a year.

As directors of the company, Nels and his associates have noticed how the expansion and retrenchment cycles have affected the price of the stock. In expansion years, profits are low, and local stockholders sell their shares; in retrenchment years, profits are high. It has become a common practice, therefore, for the directors of the company to purchase as much stock as they can afford in the year following an expansion annual report, when the price is low, and to sell that stock the

©Winston Press, Inc. Permission is given to reproduce this page for student use. 117

following year, after high profits have attracted public attention and sometimes nearly doubled the price of the stock. Some of the directors have even borrowed money to purchase stock just before a good report was released, taken advantage of the quick rise in the price of the stock, and then sold it—at a profit—to repay their loans.

The cycle of high and low stock prices has long been a matter of pure chance, since expansion and retrenchment have come in separate years. At a recent meeting of the Board of Directors, however, the treasurer and the internal auditors suggested that this situation might be made even more useful to the directors if it was more closely managed. Specifically, they suggested that four things be done:

1. That the cycle of expansion and retrenchment be managed so that these phases would fall precisely within calendar years. (This has happened primarily by chance in the past.)

2. That the President's Annual Report to stockholders be written so that it would encourage investment after retrenchment years, but offer a poor account of the company in expansion years.

3. That the auditor use different methods of accounting during alternate years, one that would give the best showing of profits for retrenchment years, and one that would emphasize expenditures and not losses for expansion years.

4. That all public relations, advertising, and news releases be written in such a way as to show the firm to have high profits and good prospects in retrenchment years, but to be in "financial trouble" in expansion years.

If you were Nels Swenson, would you approve this plan?

The Rational Strategy

Three Cases: "The Candy Store," "The Supervisor," and "Foreign Contributions"

The following cases are designed for use with the Rational Strategy, which is outlined on pages 43-50. Other Rational Strategy cases in this <u>Handbook</u> which can be used in this unit

118 © Winston Press, Inc. Permission is given to reproduce this page for student use.

include "The Sloppy Chef Layoff," page 99; "Oil Profits," page 99; "Lost and Found," page 46; "Model T," page 151; and "The Dream House," page 152.

THE CANDY STORE

A group of small boys got into the habit of going to Mr. Green's candy store every day after school. At first, everything was all right; soon, however, they began to take candy and other items without paying for them.

One day, Mr. Green caught them in the act. When he questioned them, they admitted that they'd been taking things without paying for them for quite a while. They were boys from the neighborhood and had known and liked Mr. Green for a long time. Mr. Green liked them, too.

Mr. Green didn't know whether to report them to the police, spank them and send them home, call their parents, make them pay for what they had taken, or make them work at odd jobs for him until they had paid him back.

What should he do, and why?

THE SUPERVISOR

In addition to managing his own real estate business, Jim Staffano manages a commercial building owned by his father. Four years ago, he hired Jack Davis as maintenance supervisor. Within the last two months, Jim has discovered that Jack has been stealing minor supplies from some of the tenants. The losses haven't included any items of great value, but they have been fairly regular. It seems as if Jack has simply been taking other people's things home with him.

Jim can't legally prove that Jack has been stealing, but he is absolutely sure that he has been. He now feels that he must dismiss Jack before the problem goes any further or becomes generally known; he doesn't want the reputation of the building to be jeopardized. He fears that if he tells Jack the real reason for his dismissal, though, Jack may let the reason be known and possibly take legal action against him.

Jim wants to take action on the problem. On the other hand, Jack is well liked by most of the tenants and has been a personal friend of Jim's.

What should Jim do, and why?

©Winston Press, Inc. Permission is given to reproduce this page for student use.

You are the overseas manager of a large corporation with responsibility for sales in a South American country. You believe that it's possible to bribe the government officials in that country in order to gain an advantage over your competitors in marketing your firm's products. You're sure that other firms are engaged in making similar payments, and that refusing to do the same would endanger your company's position and may even cost you your job.

What alternatives are open to you? What consequences might you expect in each case?

The Concept Strategy

Private property may not immediately come to mind when one thinks of important moral concepts, but it's really quite significant as the value around which many business and economic decisions revolve. Private ownership of property is a value established by law in most Western societies. The materials included here for the Explanation, Identification, and Modeling of the concept of property follow the procedures of the Concept Strategy outlined on pages 56-70.

Explanation

Dictionaries generally define property as the ownership, legal title, and/or control, use, and rights to dispose of material objects. Examples of property might include land and buildings (real estate); automobiles (legal title required); corporate stocks; patents on inventions; copyrights (on writings and music); mineral rights; and the right of way (use without ownership). Counter-examples (things that can't be owned) might include people (slavery is illegal); air; sunlight (solar energy); oceans, lakes, and rivers; and common property (such as government-owned parks, buildings, libraries, and museums).

Legal protection of private property is an important aspect of the concept; as the Fourteenth Amendment to the

United States Constitution states, "...nor shall any State deprive any person of life, liberty, or property, without due process of law."

Identification

"Questions of Property": A Class Discussion
The following collection of questions is generally sufficient for a 45-minute discussion. They raise the issue of the absolute private ownership of property according to both moral and legal perspectives.

• Is it morally/legally right to take food (property) when one is starving?

• Should a person have the right to block sunlight (for example, by constructing a tall building) from someone else's property?

• Should someone have the right to dam up a stream flowing through his or her property?

• Does ownership of pets give a person the right to kill the animals? To beat or torture them?

• If a person has an apple tree and the branches extend over someone else's fence, who owns the apples on that side?

• If a person builds a house on someone else's land by mistake, should the other person be able to claim it as his or her own?

• On a small island where wood is used for fuel, one woman owns all of the woodlands and will sell wood only at a high price. Do the other residents have a moral claim against her? Should they be able to do anything to make her monopoly illegal?

• Owners of a corporation employing 2,000 workers decide to relocate the firm in an area 3,000 miles away, where labor and energy are cheaper. Do the workers have any moral claim against the corporation? Do they have any legal claim?

• Should it be legal for a man to will all of his property and money to someone else (such as the local hospital), leaving his wife with no means of support?

• Should the owner of a restaurant be legally required to serve Black people or other minorities? If so, should the same law hold true for private country club membership?

Discussion of any of the above brief cases may turn into an extended debate, and the teacher may choose to move to a Debate Strategy (see pages 33-42) or simply to facilitate the discussion by continuing to pose the same question until differences of opinion are clarified. This can then be followed by an attempt to resolve the differences or to reach some sort of class compromise.

"Planning a Utopian Society":
An Exercise for Small-Group Discussions
The discussion questions above may raise enough problems concerning law and property rights for students to face the more general question, <u>What laws should a society have regarding private property?</u>

The class should be divided into small groups (from four to six students). They will be cast in the roles of organizers of their own Utopian Societies. This will involve writing laws covering four or five of the more important issues raised in the above questions.

<u>Class Instructions:</u> Create the perfect society you would like to live in by writing laws on the following topics:
1. Protection of animals.
2. Monopolies—corporate or private.
3. Membership in private clubs.
4. Use of natural resources (such as water, coal, and timber).
You may, of course, add or substitute other topics of your choosing.

Modeling

The following chart is only a starter. The facilitating questions for concept modeling are found on page 72.

The Game Strategy

"Used Cars": A Simulation

This exercise falls somewhere between a simulation and a role play. Because it can be managed, elaborated on, and adapted in many ways, only the basic outline will be included here. (The

Sample Concept Modeling Worksheet:

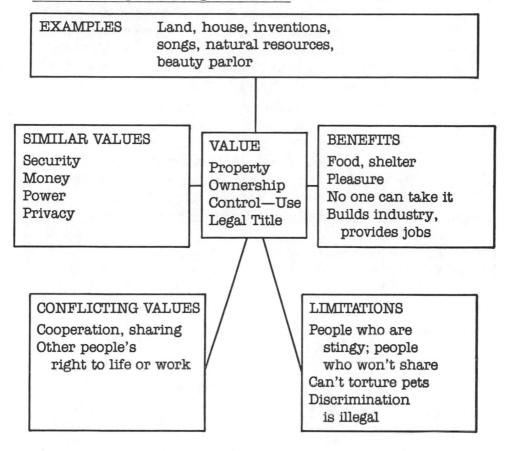

teacher may wish to consult the description of the Game Strategy found on pages 77-88.)

Situation: A used-car lot with a number of cars for sale.

Players: Two to four customers, two salespeople, two mechanics, and one business manager.

   1.   The customers are asked to leave the room while the salespeople, mechanics, and business manager set up the business.

   2.   While they are out (this may take some time), the class decides on the cars that will be for sale (at least six). These are listed on the chalkboard; students make up the descriptions. Each car is given a price.

3.   A card is made out for each car, listing some of its defects. Three or more defects should be listed for each car. The defects are not listed on the chalkboard, however; only on the cards, which the salespeople will keep. The teacher should see to it that each car has a sufficient number of defects—major ones in some cases, minor ones in others.

4.   The two mechanics are stationed off to one side. The salespeople are instructed that they can ask the mechanics' help in understanding a car's good points and defects if a customer has any questions that the salespeople aren't sure about. The salespeople may show their defect cards to the mechanics, but not to the customers. (This allows the salespeople and the mechanics to decide just what the customer will and won't be told.)

Directions to the salespeople: Remember that if you aren't sure what to say, you can ask the customer to wait while you talk with the mechanics.

5.   The salespeople are instructed that when a customer decides to buy a car, he or she should be brought to the business manager to complete the deal.

6.   The customers are then asked to return to the room and view the cars that are for sale. They can spend as much money as they want but should try to make sensible purchases. (By this time, they may have been out of the room long enough to be suspicious; this should make them inquisitive customers.)

7.   The rest of the class is instructed to listen closely to what is said during the scene.

8.   After all of the car sales have been completed, the teacher reads aloud to the customers the defects listed on the cards. If customers have purchased cars with major defects, the teacher can also describe an event that takes place shortly after the purchase. For example:

• Your car had poor brakes and they failed to hold on a hill. The car went into the guard rail—$600 damage.
• The valves were blown in the engine and you now have to pay $300 for repairs.
• The rear fenders have rusted out—$180 each.

9.   If they wish, the customers may return to the used-car salesroom to see whether they can get the Business

Manager to make the repairs or at least pay for part of them. The Business Manager should be instructed only to make an agreement to pay for part of the repairs if he or she feels that the customers were actually told something false about the cars. The law says that if the customer asks, he or she must be told the truth; if the customer doesn't ask, it's his or her problem.

Follow-up Questions
- What can happen when the truth is withheld?
- Do salespeople generally tell the truth?
- What's the best policy for a used-car business to follow?
- Is there ever a time when a salesperson should feel a responsibility to warn a customer about something, even if the customer doesn't ask?

Chapter 9:
Honesty: A Humanities Unit

This is primarily a "concept" unit, the aim of which is to move students' thinking from the concrete to the abstract, from particular cases to value concepts. The materials include a number of individual cases which have a common theme of either truth-telling or deception; they also include some passages and quotations for analysis and discussion which lead to the consideration of moral principles relevant to the cases.

The intended progression from the concrete to the abstract is one that needs to be made more than once for most students. The teacher may find it necessary to move back and forth between the discussion of principles and the consideration of cases, according to what the class is ready for or willing to try at a particular time. Students may want to move to a more abstract level right in the middle of an exercise, and the teacher may have to switch strategies halfway through a session.

To gain this flexibility, the teacher may find it helpful to become familiar with the section entitled "Comparing Moral Principles": A Class Discussion, page 144, and be prepared to turn to any of the principles for brief mention or for class discussion as the need arises.

The Awareness Strategy

"Personal Experiences": An Icebreaker

First as a whole class, and then in small groups (of four or five students each), students can open the topic by sharing their memories of times when someone has told them a lie or when they've told a lie to someone else. Examples of common "social" lies, along with one or two examples from the teacher's own experiences, can serve to break the ice. The most

For help in the development of this unit, I wish to thank Mrs. Janet Rodriguez and her former students at Wheeling High School, Wheeling, West Virginia.

common ones include the lie to get out of accepting an invitation ("I'm sorry we can't come, but Jack's sister is coming over") and the lie for the sake of being polite ("That is a nice color for the kitchen! Orange is so cheerful, isn't it?").

Small-group discussions will allow each student a chance to speak and to reflect on his or her own experiences. The assignment can be worded as follows:

> Working together, think of five different instances when someone has told a lie. Try to make them as different as you can.

As a class summary, a chalkboard list can be made of the lies that are reported, and arrows can be drawn between those that are similar. The teacher might also want to be prepared to mention some of the other types of lies discussed in this unit.

Clarifying and Defining the Concept

The following questions can either be addressed to the whole class or used as a small-group-discussion assignment (if the students have acquired small-group-discussion skills). They focus attention on the problem of defining a "lie" by distinguishing lies from other problems of communciation. It may be best if the teacher gives the small groups two or three of these questions at a time, convenes the entire class for a summary of the findings, and then repeats the process with two more questions.

Any or all of these questions may lead into an extended class discussion; it simply isn't possible to tell ahead of time which will and which won't. In conducting the class summary discussion, it's a good idea for the teacher to be prepared either to continue the discussion of any one of these questions as long as students are interested or to move right on to the next one. In addition, any or all of them could be used as a writing assignment.

- What is a "white lie"?
- Is it a lie to allow another person to believe something that's false without correcting him or her?

The materials in this unit are presented sequentially, beginning with awareness activities which introduce the topic and ending with conceptual abstractions. They can be used in any order, however, according to the teacher's approach or the demands of the course in which they are included.

- What's the difference between a lie and a mistake? Is it right to hold a person responsible for a mistake?
- Can a person tell a lie without meaning to?
- Is it a lie if someone is forced to say something he or she doesn't mean (for example, at gunpoint)?
- Is a fairy tale a lie?
- Is it possible to tell a lie to yourself?

"Opinions on Truth"

The next two worksheets contain basically the same questions. In the second, however, the tables are turned, and students are asked to judge whether they themselves would want to be treated as they've said they would treat others.

After students have completed the first worksheet, they may be asked to discuss their opinions in small groups (of four or five students) and to attempt to come to some agreement on the answers. The second worksheet can be given to them while they're in the discussion groups.

The Debate Strategy

Often, students can easily think of a number of things that can be said either to avoid telling the truth directly or to qualify it in certain ways. The Debate Strategy, therefore, is more difficult to use than the Rational Strategy with cases of truth or falsehood, since it requires clear yes or no positions. In fact, the more students become accustomed to these moral education strategies, the more they seem to want to consider many alternatives before making a choice. A division of opinion can usually be obtained, however, if the teacher insists that the person facing the problem either has to tell the truth or not.

The outline for the Debate Strategy is found on pages 33-42. Other Debate Strategy cases in this Handbook that can be used as Truthfulness exercises include "Broken Windows," page 96; "Beauty Parlor," page 115; "Breaking a Lease," page 117; "The Late Request," page 149; and "Father Tony," page 148.

OPINIONS ON TRUTH: WORKSHEET I

Circle the word after each statement which is closest to
<u>your own</u> opinion.

1. It's all right to tell a lie to keep from hurting someone
else's feelings.

Always   Often   Sometimes   Never

2. It's all right to tell a lie if it saves the person you're
speaking to from harm.

Always   Often   Sometimes   Never

3. It's all right to tell a lie if it doesn't really hurt anyone.

Always   Often   Sometimes   Never

4. It's all right to tell a lie to protect a friend.

Always   Often   Sometimes   Never

130 © Winston Press, Inc. Permission is given to reproduce this page for student use.

OPINIONS ON TRUTH: WORKSHEET II

Circle the word after each statement which is closest to
your own opinion.

1. It's all right for someone else to tell you a lie to keep from hurting your feelings.

Always   Often   Sometimes   Never

2. It's all right for someone to tell you a lie if it saves you from harm.

Always   Often   Sometimes   Never

3. It's all right for someone to tell you a lie if it doesn't really hurt anyone.

Always   Often   Sometimes   Never

4. It's all right for someone to tell you a lie to protect you.

Always   Often   Sometimes   Never

©Winston Press, Inc. Permission is given to reproduce this page for student use. 131

Three Cases: "A Doctor's Choice," "Secret Base," and "The Orphan"

Often, the decision between telling the truth and telling a lie is a very difficult one to make. There are circumstances in which it seems easier, or better, or kinder to tell a lie. The first and third cases in this section, "A Doctor's Choice" and "The Orphan," are examples of situations like these. In the first case, a doctor must decide whether or not to tell a patient that he has cancer. In the second, a grandmother must choose the best time in which to tell a boy that both of his parents have died in an accident.

Discussion questions like the ones below will help to facilitate student understanding of these complex cases. They should be used <u>following</u> the conclusion of each debate.

Questions for "A Doctor's Choice"
- If the doctor told you that your mother had cancer and was expected to live only about six months, would you tell her?
- If you yourself had some disease and had only a short time to live, would you want to know about it?
- Does a person have a right to know his or her own medical condition? Should he or she have to claim this right?
- Sooner or later, Mr. Morris will probably find out about his condition. What will happen to his relationship with Dr. Ramos if he discovers that he hasn't been told the truth?

Questions for "The Orphan"
- Is there a way to tell Billy about the death of his parents little by little? How would you do it? [This question might be most effective as a role play.]
- Should Billy be allowed to attend the funeral?
- Does Billy have a right to know immediately about his parents' deaths?
- If he weren't allowed to attend the funeral, would he possibly resent his grandmother later for not telling him and not allowing him to attend?

A DOCTOR'S CHOICE

Dr. Ramos had been taking care of Mr. Morris for a number of years. Mr. Morris was about fifty-five years old and had suffered a fairly severe heart attack three years ago, after which he was kept in bed for two months and only gradually allowed to resume his activities. Dr. Ramos had insisted that Mr. Morris avoid anything that might get him excited or upset, since there was one occasion when Mr. Morris had gone to a football game and ended up being put to bed for a couple of days with very high blood pressure. Dr. Ramos had told him then that he would have to avoid excitement in the future.

When Mr. Morris developed a tumor on his throat that Dr. Ramos thought might be malignant (cancer), the question of an operation was raised. After consulting with a specialist, Dr. Ramos advised Mr. Morris to go ahead with the operation, although he was quite concerned about Mr. Morris' heart condition. Mr. Morris was especially upset when Dr. Ramos told him about the tumor; he was worried that he might have cancer.

Dr. Ramos told him that he didn't really believe it was cancer but merely a tumor which needed to be removed. He didn't want Mr. Morris to get upset before the operation, and besides, he wasn't absolutely sure that it was cancer.

The laboratory report at the time of the operation showed that the tumor was malignant, but Dr. Ramos was quite confident that the surgery had removed all of it. The tumor had been detected quite early, and the rate of success for this particular type of operation is very high.

When Mr. Morris regained consciousness after the operation, the first thing he asked Dr. Ramos was whether or not he had cancer. Dr. Ramos noticed that Mr. Morris looked afraid, and remembering Mr. Morris' heart condition, he wondered whether or not he should tell him the truth.

Should he?

SECRET BASE

The United States has a secret missile base in the small Middle Eastern country of Morabonia. If the enemy doesn't

©Winston Press, Inc. Permission is given to reproduce this page for student use. 133

know about it, they won't put up a defense system against it; if they find out, however, the base will be useless. If the Senate Foreign Relations committee is told about the base, it's almost certain that everyone will know about it soon after.

The Committee is considering the possibility of making certain trade agreements with Morabonia and wants to know all about American involvement there. In an effort to find the information they need, the Committee Chairman asks the President whether or not we have any military bases in Morabonia.

Should the President tell him the truth?

THE ORPHAN

Billy was staying with his grandmother while his parents were away. They had all celebrated his sixth birthday before his parents had left; there had been a family dinner at McDonald's, Billy's favorite place, and a visit to the zoo with two of his friends.

Billy's parents were on their way to Los Angeles. His father had business there, and while his mother didn't usually accompany him at such times, this trip combined business with pleasure—they were celebrating their tenth anniversary.

There was nothing mysterious about the crash; a small private plane had simply taxied onto the runway before it was given clearance. In the light fog, the pilot of the commercial airliner couldn't have seen the private plane until it was too late. All thirty-four passengers were killed, as well as the crew of five and the pilot of the private plane.

Billy would have to be told, of course, but his grandmother wondered if there weren't some way that she could break the news to him little by little. It was such an awful thing for him to have to take all at once. On the other hand, she had already delayed one day, hardly able to think about it herself, and the funeral would be on the following day.

If Billy was going to be allowed to attend the funeral, she would have to tell him right away.

Should she?

134 ©Winston Press, Inc. Permission is given to reproduce this page for student use.

The Rational Strategy

Three Cases: "A Day Off," "The Prom," and "The Clay Pit"

The cases which follow are designed for use with the general outline of the Rational Strategy found on pages 43-50. Since questions of truth-telling are a part of everyone's experience, it may be especially appropriate here to ask students to make up cases of their own, either in class or during a writing assignment.

Other Rational Strategy cases in this Handbook which are appropriate for this unit include "Rocky Tomatoes," page 179; "Randy's I.Q. Test," page 153; "The Dream House," page 152; and "The Supervisor," page 119.

A DAY OFF

Ella has been very sick for over a year. Sometimes she feels all right, but at other times, without warning, she suffers from dizzy spells.

The doctor hasn't been able to determine the cause of her dizziness and has ordered her to go directly to the hospital for tests the next time she has a spell. Sam, Ella's husband, has already taken a number of days off work when his wife was too ill to be left alone. The absence days he's allowed for "personal reasons," however, have run out.

One morning, as Sam is about to leave for work, Ella feels dizzy again. Sam knows that he really should take her to the hospital, but he also knows that if he takes another day off for "personal reasons" he may lose his job.

He considers calling in to work to say that he himself is sick; he doesn't think his boss would question him about it.

What should Sam do?

THE PROM

Mary, a sophomore in high school, has recently started dating Bill, a star on the football team and the class vice-president. The Junior Prom is about a month away, and Mary thinks that Bill will probably ask her to go with him.

Before he does, however, a boy she's known for a long time, John, asks if she'll go to the Prom with him. Mary has always liked John as a friend—they're neighbors, and have always gone to school together—, so she doesn't want to hurt his feelings, but she'd really rather go to the Prom with Bill if he asks her.

What should Mary do?

THE CLAY PIT

Craig and his friends, who are all about fourteen or fifteen years old, have a secret swimming place—a deserted clay pit on the outskirts of town. There used to be a "No Trespassing" sign on the road into it, but it fell down a few years earlier. Craig had mentioned the clay pit to his parents—without saying anything about swimming—, and his father had told him never to go near it. But Craig had continued to go along with his friends anyway; some of their parents knew where they were swimming and approved. For most of the summer, Craig had just told his parents that he was "going swimming" without telling them where. His parents apparently thought he was going to the public swimming pool.

One day Craig had an accident while he was swimming at the clay pit. Under the water on one side of the pit was some abandoned machinery, part of an old shovel that had been left when the pit filled with water. The boys never dove into the water from that side, but Craig had forgotten about it. During a game of water tag, he dove straight onto the tallest part of the submerged machinery and hit his shoulder and head. The scrape on his shoulder wasn't too bad, but his head ached for quite a while.

Craig didn't tell his parents about this accident because he was afraid they might not let him go out with his friends at all any more. A week later, however, he was still having headaches at times, and he began to worry. Since he had always liked and trusted their family doctor, Dr. Foster, he decided to ask him about it.

Dr. Foster told Craig that he thought the headaches would go away soon, and that Craig would be all right. When he asked him how he had hurt himself, Craig felt that he had to tell the truth—and did.

136 ©Winston Press, Inc. Permission is given to reproduce this page for student use.

"But," he added, "I didn't tell my parents about it. You won't tell my parents, will you? You know how strict they are, and it really was an accident. I know how to take care of myself pretty well, and I've never really done anything wrong. But I don't always tell my parents everything because they're so strict and don't trust me. That's one of the problems of being an only child when your parents are older than most kids' parents; they don't always understand. I'll be all right, so you don't have to tell them, do you?"

If you were Dr. Foster, what would you say?

The Concept Strategy

"Telling the Truth to Children": Topics for Class Discussion

This collection of questions brings together a number of instances during which something <u>less</u> than the whole truth —or something <u>more</u> than it—is commonly told to young children. The questions can be used all together for a single discussion, or each one can be role played as a separate case. They should help to focus attention on what the word <u>lie</u> means.

- Is it a lie to tell little children about Santa Claus?
- Is it dishonest to let little children believe in fairy tales <u>as though they were true? Are all fictional stories lies?</u>
- Should a child be told that <u>he or she is adopted? If so, when, and at what age?</u>
- Should <u>young</u> children be told about sex? If so, when, how, <u>and by whom?</u>

"Famous Quotations": Topics for Discussion

For class discussion, small-group discussion, or writing assignments, students can be asked to explain the meanings of some of the following quotations:

- <u>Sin has many tools, but a lie is the handle which fits them all.</u>
  Oliver Wendell Holmes

©Winston Press, Inc. Permission is given to reproduce this page for student use. 137

- The world is naturally averse to all the truth it sees or hears but swallows nonsense and a lie with greediness and gluttony.

  Samuel Butler

- One of the most startling differences between a cat and a lie is that a cat has only nine lives.

  Mark Twain

- The great masses of people will more easily fall victim to a great lie than to a small one.

  Adolf Hitler

- Half the truth is often a great lie.

  Ben Franklin

- He that tells a lie to save his credit, wipes his mouth with his sleeve to save his napkin.

  Thomas Overbury

- The cruelest lies are often told in silence.

  Robert Louis Stevenson

- You can't believe half the lies you hear, but you have to believe some of them.

  Uncle Billy O'Brien

Honesty: Concept Modeling

The modeling technique of the Concept Strategy is outlined on pages 51-76 of Part II. The Facilitating Questions are found on page 72. The following chart is just a starter.

"Principles of Honesty": A Philosophical Approach

Philosophers have often dealt with the moral issues of honesty and deception and have held different views of when deception is and isn't justified. Viewed from one perspective, the positions of various philosophers can be considered as justifications for possible exceptions to the general rule of honesty.

Sample Concept Modeling Worksheet:

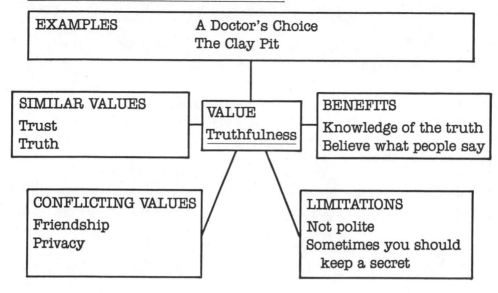

The teacher might want to attempt an analysis of the writings of various philosophers on the issue with better students. A number of such passages are excerpted on pages 141-143 following. Many young people haven't yet attained much capability in abstract thinking, however, so the teacher may have to interpret the excerpts line by line. They are relatively short, though, and should prove well worth the effort. It will be helpful if each student has his or her own copy of whichever quotation is being discussed at the time.

Discussion questions like the ones which follow will help to facilitate student understanding of these concepts.

Questions for "The Ninth Commandment"
- What does "false witness" mean?
- Would Calvin think that "cultivating genuine truth" means that we should never keep secrets from one another?
- What reasons does Calvin give for considering slander wrong?
- Do you think this means that you should never say anything bad about another person?
- People often lie and then say, "I didn't mean any harm by it." Do you think that Calvin would accept this excuse?

Questions for "The Lie in Self-Defense"
• What relationship does Schopenhauer see between deception and violence?
• Schopenhauer says that one may lie in self-defense if it's more convenient. Would it ever be better to use force than to lie?
• What might Schopenhauer mean by the "strict observance" of self-defense? Is it self-defense to "get" the other person before he or she "gets" you? [Example: The Arab-Israeli war of 1967.]
• If someone says that he lied to his mother in self-defense because "She would kill me if she knew the truth," is this a valid justification?

Questions for "Truthfulness"
• Does everyone have a "right to know" and a "right to truth"?
• If a person doesn't have a "right to know" in a certain case, would this justify deceiving him or her?
• Is it possible to "speak the truth" and still deceive another person? Is keeping silent a justifiable way out of a problem?
• Are there other natural abilities human beings have which it would be wrong to abuse?
• Is the "argument from the social nature of man" a correct one? If a person believes that there are some few times when lying is morally justified, what would he or she say to the argument that "You could never tell when a person is lying and when he is not"?

Questions for "Valuational Conflicts Between Truthfulness and the So-Called 'Necessary Lie'"
• Do you agree that Hartmann's situations place before a person the "unescapable alternatives" he says they do?
• Is his statement that "value stands against value" the best way of analyzing situations in which people sometimes say that it's all right to lie? What exactly are the values which stand against each other in the situations he describes?
• What does Hartmann imply by saying that these questions cannot be solved "theoretically"?
• Do you agree that the person who tells a lie takes upon himself or herself the guilt involved in violating this value?

THE NINTH COMMANDMENT*
by John Calvin

Since God, who is truth, rejects falsehood, we must cultivate genuine truth towards each other.

By vicious slander, we sin against our neighbor's good name: by lying, sometimes even by casting a slur upon him, we injure him.

The legitimate observance of this commandment consists in employing the tongue in the maintenance of truth so as to promote both the good name and the prosperity of our neighbor.

The justice of this is perfectly clear. For if a good name is more precious than riches (as it says in the Bible: Proverbs 22:1), a man, in being robbed of his good name, is no less injured than if he were robbed of his goods.

THE LIE IN SELF-DEFENSE**
by Arthur Schopenhauer

Accordingly, there are two ways of doing wrong, those of violence and those of deception. Just as by violence I can kill another, or rob him, or force him to obey me, so too by means of deception I can do all these things....

But just as I can repel force by force without doing wrong, so I can repel force by deception if I lack the power, or if it appears more convenient to me. Therefore, in cases where I have a right to use force, I also have a right to tell lies....

However, this limitation to the case of self-defense must be strictly observed...for in itself the lie is a very dangerous instrument.

---

*John Calvin, Institutes of the Christian Religion, Book II, Chapter VII, Paragraph 47(1559). Adapted from the translation by H. Beveridge (Grand Rapids: Wm. B. Eerdmans, 1962), pages 352-353.

**Arthur Schopenhauer, On the Basis of Morality, Section 17. Adapted from the translation of E.F.J. Payne (Indianapolis, Indiana: The Bobbs-Merrill Co., Inc., 1965), pages 158-161.

©Winston Press, Inc. Permission is given to reproduce this page for student use. 141

TRUTHFULNESS
by Austin Fagothey, S.J.

Man has not only a right to be but a right to know, not only a right to life but a right to truth. He demands respect for his own intellect and must show similar respect for his neighbor's intellect by putting right order in the communications between his own mind and the minds of others. He who speaks is obliged to speak the truth.

1. Argument from the abuse of a natural ability.

It is natural to intelligent beings to have some means of communicating their thoughts so as to win assent from others. But to communicate as thought what is not thought, to convey seriously to another as true what one knows to be untrue, is to abuse this means of communication and to render it unfit for its purpose. Hence lying is an act against man's nature and a violation of the natural law.

2. Argument from the social nature of man.

Human society is built on mutual trust and faith among men. But if lying were morally allowed, we could never tell when a person is lying and when he is not....His speech would cease to have any meaning for us, and, if this practice became widespread, there would be an end to human communication and thus to human society.

VALUATIONAL CONFLICTS BETWEEN TRUTHFULNESS AND THE SO-CALLED "NECESSARY LIE"
by Nicholai Hartmann

Truthfulness as a value, with its specific moral claim, admits of no exceptions at all. What is called the necessary lie is always an anti-value—at least from the point of view of truthfulness as a value. No end can justify deliberate deception as a means—certainly not in the sense of causing it to cease to be a moral wrong.

Still we are confronted with a very serious moral problem, which is by no means solved by the simple rejection of each and every lie. There are situations which place before a

From Austin Fagothey, Right and Reason, 4th ed. (St. Louis: The C.V. Mosby Co., 1967), pages 252-255.

142 ©Winston Press, Inc. Permission is given to reproduce this page for student use.

man the unescapable alternative either of sinning against truthfulness or against some other equally high, or even some higher, value. A physician violates his professional duty, if he tells a patient who is dangerously ill the critical state of his health; the imprisoned soldier who, when questioned by the enemy, allows the truth about his country's tactics to be extorted from him, is guilty of high treason; a friend, who does not try to conceal information given to him in strictest personal confidence, is guilty of breach of confidence. In all cases the mere virtue of silence is not adequate. Where suspicions are aroused, mere silence may be extremely eloquent. If the physician, the prisoner, the posessor of confidential information will do their duty of warding off a calamity that threatens, they must resort to a lie. But if they do so, they make themselves guilty on the side of truthfulness.

It is a portentous error to believe that such questions may be solved theoretically. Every attempt of the kind is a one-sided and inflexible rigorism concerning one value at the expense of the rest. The examples cited are so chosen that truthfulness always seems to be inferior to the other value which is placed in opposition to it. It is the morally mature and seriously minded person who is here inclined to decide in favour of the other value and to take upon himself the responsibility for the lie. For it is inherent in the essence of such moral conflicts that in them value stands against value and that is not possible to escape from them without being guilty. The conflict arises from the structure of the situation. This makes it impossible to satisfy both at the same time.

Nevertheless, a man who is in such a situation cannot avoid making a decision. What a man ought to do, when he is confronted with a serious conflict that is fraught with responsibility, is this: to decide according to his best conscience; that is, according to his own living sense of the relative height of the respective values, and to take upon himself the consequences, external as well as inward, ultimately the guilt involved in the violation of the one value. He ought to carry the guilt and in so doing become stronger, so that he can carry it with pride. Real moral life is not such that one can stand guiltless in it.

From Nicholai Hartmann, <u>Ethics</u> (London: 1932), Volume II, pages 283-285.

©Winston Press, Inc. Permission is given to reproduce this page for student use.

"Comparing Moral Principles": A Class Discussion

Although the following discussion format draws together some of the moral principles expressed in the philosophical excerpts above, it may also be used independently of them.

The basic plan of this discussion is to view the various moral principles mentioned and illustrated throughout this unit as establishing exceptions to the value of honesty. By comparing these principles with one another, students can learn to evaluate the pros and cons of each and begin to develop the notion of a moral principle as a rule to be applied to all cases.

Step 1.   To begin with, the value of honesty as an accepted social value should be established. The common maxim "Honesty is the best policy" can be used here, since it's usually understood as meaning that for the most part and in general it's right to be honest. Most students will accept this, although a few, it seems, will always want to bring up the exceptions discussed in earlier cases.

The nature of this maxim should be discussed (Is honesty the best policy?) until students are satisfied with it. And they'll stay satisfied as long as they understand that they'll be allowed to make some exceptions. When there is general agreement among the students, the maxim "Honesty is the best policy" can be written on the chalkboard.

(Note: In this discussion, the terms value and justify appear as important moral words. The teacher should be prepared, if necessary, to spend some time on each of these terms as they arise. The term principle appears here as well, but it can more easily be left to acquire its own meaning through use.)

Step 2.   The following statements are philosophical principles which have been said at different times and by different philosophers to justify exceptions to the policy of honesty. The teacher can read these aloud, distribute them, project them on an overhead projector, or write them on the chalkboard one at a time. With each principle, discussion should center on these three questions:

- What does the principle say, and what does it mean?
- Does the principle apply to any of the cases that are listed as possible exceptions to honesty as the best policy?
- Do you agree with the principle? Do you think that following this principle might sometimes be wrong?

Principle I: Concern for Others.

Lies are seldom justified if they're told for the speaker's own good. A lie is justified only if it helps someone else.

Principle II: No Right to Know.

In most cases, people do have a right to know the truth. But in a case where a person has no right to know something, it's justified to tell him or her a lie. We often say, for example, "It's none of his business."

Principle III: To Protect Other Values.

Honesty is an important value; we want to trust others and have them trust us. But other values—such as life, freedom, and friendship—are also important and may sometimes be lost due to absolute honesty. Deception is justified only if some other important value could otherwise be lost.

Principle IV: Self-Defense.

In any case where a person would be justified in using force to defend himself or herself, he or she would also be justified in telling a lie. But the only time a lie is justified is in a genuine case of self-defense, not just when someone wants to avoid embarrassment or escape punishment.

Principle V: Never Tell a Lie.

Some people, of course, don't believe that any exceptions are justified. What if people made exceptions whenever they pleased?

As these principles are discussed, they can be added to the chalkboard or projection chart as "possible exceptions."

When completed, the chalkboard diagram should look something like the following:

PRINCIPLES

VALUE

Honesty is
the best policy

Possible
Exceptions

I   Concern for Others
II No Right to Know
III To Protect Other Values
IV Self-Defense
V   Never Tell a Lie

To reinforce the concept, students can be asked again to state a case that would be an instance of each principle. It should be made clear, however, that people disagree about these exceptions.

Step 3.   As a final step, students can be asked to discuss which of the five principles for possible exceptions they feel to be the best one and why. It may be better, however, if they're asked to do this as a writing assignment first to allow them more time for individual reflection. When different students defend different principles, it will be clear how moral perspectives can differ among people who still believe that morality is a matter of values and principles.

The Game Strategy

The simulation "Used Cars," included in the unit on Property, pages 122-125, is well suited to the issues raised in this unit and is suggested for use here.

Chapter 10:
Integrity: A Behavioral Sciences Unit

Dictionaries define <u>integrity</u> as <u>completeness</u> or <u>unity</u>. Recently, the concept has come to signify the notion of the wholeness of the individual as a person. In past generations, moral philosophers have used the term <u>dignity</u> to refer to the same notion.

It is especially appropriate to deal with the value of integrity as the central focus for moral education in behavioral science courses because the social sciences have recently been criticized on a number of counts (sometimes rightly, sometimes wrongly) for ignoring the personal dignity of individuals. The counseling profession, which ought to have the wholeness of the individual as its goal, has been taken to task for keeping records on people with little regard for the privacy of this information. Sociologists have been accused of manipulating people to attain social goals—for example, in advocating school busing to attain racial integration. And researchers have been criticized for ignoring the effects of their experiments on their willing, and sometimes unwilling, subjects.

The Debate Strategy

Three Cases: "Father Tony," "The Late Request," and "Keeping the Peace"

The cases in the first part of this unit are designed to raise the questions of how much people should know about one another and how we come by such information. Follow-up questions direct students' attention to the effects of decisions on specific

The materials in this unit are presented sequentially, beginning with cases for debate which introduce the topic and ending with conceptual abstractions. They can be used in any order, however, according to the teacher's approach or the demands of the course in which they are included.

individuals; these questions are important for raising the consideration of integrity.

Other Debate Strategy cases in this Handbook which might be used in this unit include "Ms. Robin," page 97; "Not Allowed to Die," page 176; "Breaking a Lease," page 117; "A Doctor's Choice," page 133; and "A Ghost from the Past," page 34.

The Debate Strategy is discussed in Part II, pages 33-42.

FATHER TONY

Father Anthony Morelli is chaplain at State College. He's well liked by the students because he's always willing to listen to problems and give honest advice. He can usually be found in the Coffee Shop at lunch time and is never upset even when people call him or stop by his house in the middle of the night.

Father Tony got to know Doug because he had seen him often in the Coffee Shop sitting off by himself. Doug was an economics major in his junior year, but he was more interested in the Air Force Reserve Officer's Training Corps (ROTC), in which he was a drill instructor. Doug's political views were strictly conservative, almost to the point of preferring a police state—or so it seemed to Father Tony. Despite their differences of opinion on social matters, however, they became close friends. Actually, Doug had few other friends, and Father Tony suspected that he might be somewhat afraid of people in general. At times, he seemed to be terrified of everyone.

When the student protest against the ROTC began, Doug was noticeably more upset. Father Tony invited him over to the Chapel office, where they had a long talk that calmed some of Doug's fears and helped him to control his anger. In the course of the conversation, however, Doug told Father Tony that he was afraid that the protestors would attempt to take over the ROTC building and said that he thought that anyone who threatened the campus police protecting the building ought to be shot. In fact, he told Father Tony that he kept a gun in his room "just in case," although he knew that this was against dormitory regulations.

This unit was developed with the help of Mr. George Burns, Chairman of the Social Studies Department, Brooke High School, Brooke County, West Virginia.

 © Winston Press, Inc. Permission is given to reproduce this page for student use.

After Doug left his office, Father Tony wondered whether he should tell the Dean of Student Affairs about Doug's gun. He realized that Doug had told him about it in confidence, but there was always the chance that Doug's anger and fear would get the best of him and he would lose control.

Should Father Tony tell the Dean about Doug and his gun?

THE LATE REQUEST

As a reporter for the Middletown Press, you've been assigned to cover the police news. One evening, while you're at the police station copying the list of traffic violations for the day, an officer enters, accompanied by a man and a woman who are arguing.

The man, Mr. Sawyer, is a member of the city council and has represented a low-income neighborhood for the last seven years. All during that time, he has worked actively for his district. He has insisted upon school repairs and persuaded the school board to appoint a very capable principal. Because of his efforts, a park has been built in the district, and he has also obtained adequate police protection for the area, which has been neglected in the past.

The woman, who is Mrs. Sawyer, goes over to the desk and demands that she be allowed to press charges for assault against her husband. When the officer at the desk asks her what happened, she tells him that she and Mr. Sawyer had gone out to a nightclub, and when she wanted to go home he had refused to leave. They had started arguing about it, and finally Mr. Sawyer had taken her outside and pushed her toward the car. She had slipped on the curb and bumped her arm and shoulder against the car.

"I've had enough of this rough stuff," she says. "It's time George learned his lesson."

Mr. Sawyer, who does appear to be a little drunk, comes over and begs her not to sign the complaint. She tells him again that she's had enough, asks for the paper (which the officer has just completed), signs it, and storms out. The officer tells Mr. Sawyer that there's nothing he can do unless she withdraws the complaint.

©Winston Press, Inc. Permission is given to reproduce this page for student use.

After he leaves, you go to the desk and ask to see the charges to verify the names. Then you return to your office at the Press to file your report.

As you're completing your report, the telephone rings and you answer it. Mrs. Sawyer has called to tell you that she's made a big mistake in writing out a complaint against her husband. She was a little drunk, too, she says, and got carried away. Her husband hadn't really hurt her, and she has withdrawn the complaint. The officer told her, however, that it was on the public record and that the newspaper would probably report it, since it's the practice of the paper to report all charges.

She tells you that the report would ruin her husband's political career. He has been doing an exceptional job for the district, she points out, and the people of that area would have a hard time finding another representative as good as he is.

Would you report the incident?

KEEPING THE PEACE

The National Nazi Party is an extremist group which advocates that the right to vote be taken away from Black people and Jewish people. They believe in the superiority of the "white" race and have proposed that Blacks and Jews be deported from the United States to Africa and Israel.

The Party has very few followers, but it's vocal enough to elicit strong reactions from Black and Jewish organizations. At recent Nazi Party meetings, Blacks and Jews have assembled to protest. The Party members have responded by indicating that they intend to march "along with the other patriotic organizations" in the local Memorial Day parade.

In his efforts to keep law and order, the police chief has come to the conclusion that he needs to keep close surveillance on the activities of the Nazi Party. To do this, he has asked the district judge to permit him to tap the telephones of the Nazi Party chairman and secretary so that he can find out about their plans in advance and be prepared. He realizes that the Nazis haven't yet broken any laws, but he nevertheless feels sure that their activities are likely to incite riots.

If you were the judge, would you authorize the police chief to tap the Nazi Party's phones?

The Rational Strategy

Three Cases: "Model T," "The Dream House," and "Randy's I.Q. Test"

The cases which follow are designed for use with the Rational Strategy outlined on pages 43-50. The final case in this section, "Randy's I.Q. Test," leads directly into the Game Strategy and Awareness Strategy materials which follow it.

Other Rational Strategy cases in this Handbook which may be used in this unit include "The Sloppy Chef Layoff," page 99; "Sarah," page 178; "The Supervisor," page 119; and "The Prom," page 135.

MODEL T

Frank and Jim went to live at Frank's uncle's farm for the summer. They figured they could earn enough money at odd jobs in the neighborhood to support themselves. Frank's uncle lived alone in the back hills, forty miles or so from the nearest town, so the young men assumed that they wouldn't need money except to help pay for food and gas. They knew that they could easily earn that much and have time to spare.

One of the first jobs they got was that of cleaning out Mrs. McCarty's old barn. She said that she'd pay them $2 per hour each, which wasn't much; she could hardly afford more, however, since she lived on the small railroad pension her husband had left and had no other money. The barn was full of junk collected over the years, and Mrs. McCarty told them to take it all to the dump.

As they were pulling things out and loading them onto Frank's uncle's truck, Jim found an old pocket knife. One blade of the knife appeared to be a pick or an awl that had been used for leather work. Anyway, it was old, and he liked it, so he asked Mrs. McCarty if he could keep it. "Sure, keep anything ya want," she said. "I just don't know how you're goin' to drag that old car off."

Jim and Frank had never thought that she meant for them to take the old Model T to the dump! It was a real antique, worth $800 to $1,000 as it was if they could get it back home. "You don't really mean to throw out the Model T, do you?" Jim asked.

"It's no good," said Mrs. McCarty. "It hasn't run in twenty years; I don't know anyone who'd wanna ride in it anyway."

"Can we see if it'll start?" Frank asked.

"That'd take some work," she replied, "but you're welcome to play around with it on the way to the dump—as long as you don't charge me two bucks an hour for the time you spend doin' it."

When Frank and Jim went back to look at the car, they found that it was in even better condition than they thought. If they fixed it up and got it running, they could take it back home and easily sell it for $2,000. Of course, they decided to try.

They felt bad about Mrs. McCarty, though. She obviously didn't know the value of what she had given them, and they wondered if it would be fair to just take it without telling her its real value.

What should Frank and Jim do?

THE DREAM HOUSE

Mr. and Mrs. Rogers bought their "dream house" in Wintersville six years ago. It was just the sort of place they had been looking for: three bedrooms (they have two children) and a family room with a fireplace in addition to the living room. They made some improvements which were expensive—a patio in back, and a second bathroom—, but they thought they were worth the investment. Until they discovered the termites, that is.

Mr. Rogers was putting in some new electrical outlets when he found that wherever he drilled, the drill went through the beams as though they were made of cardboard. He checked around and found that all of the major beams and supports of the house were full of holes. "Termites eat away the insides," he explained later to Mrs. Rogers, "and can leave a house in ruins before anyone even notices them."

They called an exterminator, who told them that he could get rid of the termites. The damage they had already done,

152 ©Winston Press, Inc. Permission is given to reproduce this page for student use.

however, would cost thousands of dollars to repair—perhaps as much as $15,000.

When the Rogers' friend, Mr. Jones, who's a lawyer, heard about their problem, he immediately advised them to sell the house. Mrs. Rogers asked, "How could we ever find anyone to buy it with the termite damage as bad as it is?"

"Don't tell them," Mr. Jones said. "You don't <u>have</u> to tell them unless they ask you specifically about it. Perhaps the termites were here six years ago when you bought the house and the former owner did the same to you. It goes on all the time. You'd better get your money out of the place before it gets any worse."

What would you do if you were the Rogers couple?

RANDY'S I.Q. TEST

Randy is in the sixth grade. He has worked hard in school, and his teachers like him because he's always willing to work harder than most students even though he doesn't always do better.

The school grading system uses an <u>O</u> for outstanding, an <u>S</u> for satisfactory, and a <u>U</u> for unsatisfactory, each with the possibility of a plus or minus. Randy has received mostly S's and many S-minuses, with an occasional plus from a teacher who grades for effort more than achievement.

As part of the sixth-grade guidance program, Randy recently took an I.Q. test. The scoring for the test was: High, 25-30; Average, 20-25; Low, 16-20; Slow Learner, 12-15; and Mentally Retarded, 0-11. Randy got a 16.

After the tests were scored, the guidance counselor set up interviews with each of the students who had taken the test. The purpose of the interviews was to advise the students about the courses of study they might want to follow in high school and to discuss their vocational interests and abilities.

Randy's interview is this afternoon, and the counselor, Mr. Martin, is facing a problem.

Should he tell Randy that his score was very low (just above the Slow Learner category), or shouldn't he? What <u>should</u> he say?

©Winston Press, Inc. Permission is given to reproduce this page for student use. 153

The Game Strategy

Role Playing "Randy's I.Q. Test"

The case of "Randy's I.Q. Test" is good for role
playing because students will have different opinions about
what Randy, his parents, his teachers, and the school officials
should be told about his I.Q. score. The role play will focus
attention on the different ways of telling people things about
themselves and on how important this can be. Letting different
students play the part of the counselor at different times, with
discussion in between, will give students additional experience
in communciation skills and human relations.

If the case hasn't previously been used for discussion, it
should be read aloud or distributed and explained briefly. Roles
may be described as follows:

Randy's Counselor (Mr. Martin): You've given Randy a
number of tests in the past, in addition to the I.Q. test. The test
results are for your own information as counselor, and you can
choose whether or not to tell them to anyone else. You also
have copies of Randy's grade reports, an interest test which
shows that he's mechanically inclined, and a personality test
which shows that he's friendly and able to get along with
people. His primary difficulty, therefore, is his low mental
ability, and it will be your task to steer him into an appropriate
high school course of studies which will lead him toward a
career he'll be suited for.

Randy: You know that the counselor has seen the
results of your I.Q. test, and you want to know your exact
score. You're also interested in his opinion of what you should
plan to do in high school. Perhaps you're thinking of becoming
a medical technician; you'll want to ask the counselor about
this.

After the initial interview and discussion, Randy leaves,
and the following characters may enter one at a time (or two, in
the case of the parents) to speak with Mr. Martin:

Junior High Counselor: You're from the school which
Randy will be entering next fall. One of his present teachers
has suggested that Randy has a very difficult time with his

studies and should perhaps be placed in the slow learners' class. You want to find out from Mr. Martin whether or not he thinks this would be a good idea.

Randy's Principal: In completing the records which will be sent to the junior high school, you need to put down all of the information about the students that you can get. Knowing that Randy has been given some tests, and that the junior high may have to make decisions concerning his program, you would like Mr. Martin to submit his test results to you. You realize, however, that the test results belong to him as a professional counselor and that he's not obligated to submit them for school records.

Randy's Parents: You know that Randy has taken some tests and that he'll be advised about what courses he should take during junior high and high school. Your task as parents will be to help steer Randy in a direction that's good for him.

An alternative role play could include an entirely new set of parents, principal, and junior high counselor who have very different feelings and approaches. Students playing the parents, for example, could consider some of the following instructions:

Randy's Parents II: You think that Randy is pretty stupid and that he ought to be told this so he won't get his hopes up too high. You think that he may as well give up on school; perhaps he should even quit school and get a job sooner. You've told Randy this and have given him very little encouragement to do well in his studies. (This is a harder role to play, but it's what some parents are really like. You may say something right away that lets the counselor know you think Randy is stupid, such as, "We always told him he was the dumbest kid on the block.")

Randy's Parents III: You think that Randy is a capable boy and know that he's mechanically inclined. You'd like him to go on to college and have high hopes that he'll become an engineer.

Following the role play, topics for class discussion or writing assignments might include the following:
• The report Randy's counselor will have to write on his tests, and his advice to Randy.

- Randy's feelings about what he's been told, and his understanding of himself and his future.
- A speech that the counselor, Mr. Martin, will give describing the difficulties of his job.
- The uses and misuses of I.Q. tests.

The Awareness Strategy

"Personalizing the Question of Tests and Experiments"

The purpose of this activity is to encourage students to consider the implications of what people know or think about themselves. It may be used independently, but it works best if it follows either the Rational Strategy or role play use of the case of "Randy's I.Q. Test" (page 153). The case raises in an objective way—i.e., via talking about someone else—the same issues that this strategy asks students to consider when it's knowledge of themselves that's in question.

The following questions can be used for a class discussion, for small-group discussions, or for writing assignments. It may be preferable to ask students to first write a paragraph expressing their own opinions, which will then serve as the basis for the rest of the exercise.

- Would you like to know your own I.Q.?
- If you knew your I.Q., would you tell your friends what it was?
- Would you like your parents to know your I.Q.?
- Would you like your teachers to know your I.Q.?
- Would you want this information to be released to employers if you were applying for a job?
- Would you like this information to be recorded on school records?
- Would you like to see all I.Q. scores made public?

During an actual discussion of these questions, a group of students who were in favor of knowing their own I.Q. scores were strongly opposed to having these scores put in school records or made public. When asked if they would tell their closest friends, one student admitted quite frankly that he'd first try to get his friends to tell him their scores and would only divulge his own if it was higher!

A second possible stage for this strategy asks students to consider the pros and cons of knowing other information about themselves which might be determined through tests. The following real or hypothetical tests might be proposed for discussion:

- Personality tests (which might tell a student if he or she were jealous, self-centered, or possessive).
- Popularity tests (which might tell a student that he or she is less well liked by others than he or she believes).
- Mathematical or mechanical ability tests.
- Conformity tests (such as Asch experiments, which might have been discussed in class).
- Authority and obedience tests (such as the Milgram experiments, which might have been discussed in class).
- Moral development tests (which might show that one person is at a higher moral stage than another).

The Rational Strategy

"Ethical Principles in Scientific Research with Human Participants"

This activity raises the question of whether people's integrity should be respected during psychological and social research. It's appropriate for any course in which experiments or other types of research involving human subjects are being discussed, especially after students have studied specific experiments. The Game Strategy at the end of this activity, which asks students to explain the purpose and procedures of specific experiments which they've already studied while looking at them from a moral perspective, can be used as a review exercise.

The Ethical Principles and some of the case materials below are drawn from a 1972 report by the Ad Hoc Committee on Ethical Standards in Psychological Research of the American Psychological Association. A valuable resource for this unit, the report is entitled Ethical Principles in the Conduct of Research with Human Participants, and is published by the APA (1200 Seventeenth Street N.W., Washington, D.C., 20036).

The APA Guidelines and Their Use

The following is an adaptation of the ten principles established by the American Psychological Association.* They have been rephrased here to simplify the content and remove some overlap in order that they will stand out more clearly as "single-concept" guidelines. They have also been rearranged; guidelines 9 and 10, which are actually the first two in the APA report, are more effective if they're considered after the others rather than before. In fact, principle 9 covers the use of all the other guidelines: It indicates that they're not to be treated as absolute commands, but that decision-making involves a balancing of values. Principle 10 states merely that final responsibility for decisions and actions rests on the individuals implementing them; it can't be pushed off onto either a research team or a committee which approves the research.

The principles should be copied and distributed for discussion so that students can refer to them easily when considering problem cases. The pages immediately following the principles contain cases for discussion. Most have been adapted from the APA report mentioned above; some have been rewritten to eliminate technical language, while others have been expanded to illustrate specific problems. It is not implied here that these are all instances of violations of the APA principles—only that some of the guidelines apply to these cases and must be given consideration.

It would be best to discuss some of these cases with the whole class; others can then be used for small-group discussions or writing assignments. In each instance, three general questions might prove useful:

* Which of the APA principles are relevant to the case?
* Do you consider the research acceptable, or unacceptable?
* If you think it's unacceptable, what might be done instead so that the research objectives are accomplished in a morally acceptable manner?

*I wish to thank Professor Stuart W. Cook of the University of Colorado, who was chairman of the committee which prepared the APA guidelines in 1973, for his helpful advice.

ETHICAL PRINCIPLES IN SCIENTIFIC RESEARCH WITH HUMAN PARTICIPANTS

1. Participants should be informed of anything that might affect their willingness to participate. If withholding information is necesary, the investigator's responsibility to protect the dignity and integrity of participants is greater.

2. When concealment, secrecy, or deception is necessary, an explanation of this must be given to participants after the study. Participants should not be left with a general distrust of social scientists.

3. No unnecessary pressure or coercion should be put upon people to participate. Participants should be free to quit at any time. People's privacy should not be invaded. Special care should be taken when the investigator is in a position of power over the participant.

4. Acceptable research requires a clear agreement about mutual responsibilities between investigator and participants. The investigator has an obligation to keep all promises.

5. Participants should not be subjected to physical or mental discomfort, harm, or danger. If there is any risk, the participant should be informed and the danger kept to a minimum. A research procedure may not be used if it is likely to cause serious and lasting harm to the participants.

6. When the research is finished the investigator must explain the study and correct any misunderstandings that may have arisen.

7. If there are any undesirable effects on participants during the research, the investigator must do all he [or she] can to correct or remove them.

8. Information about participants must be kept confidential. If there is any danger that this may be impossible, the participant should be made aware of this fact.

9. In judging the ethical acceptability of a research plan, the investigator must weigh the human value of the advance of scientific knowledge against the effects of the research upon participants. Advice from people not directly involved in the research program may be necessary.

10. Final responsibility for the ethical acceptability of research always lies with the scientific investigator.

These principles have been adapted from Ethical Principles in the Conduct of Research with Human Participants. American Psychological Association, Copyright 1973.

©Winston Press, Inc. Permission is given to reproduce this page for student use.

RESEARCH WITH HUMAN PARTICIPANTS: I

1. In an experiment designed to test people's anxieties about failure, subjects were given a number of difficult mathematical problems to solve. The subjects were told that the problems were very simple, however, and that the investigators were only studying the speed of their calculations. Immediately following the test, the participants were told that the questions had been intentionally frustrating and were then given a simple example that might be used in a test for speed of calculation.

2. In an experiment to determine the hallucinogenic effects of LSD as compared with other drugs, participants were not told the common names (LSD, marijuana) of the drugs because it was known that if they were they'd develop expectations that would increase their tendency to hallucinate.

3. A study was designed to test driver reaction to sudden hazardous situations. The subject, who was driving, and the experimenter passed by a "construction site." At a time determined by the car's velocity, a realistic dummy was propelled in front of the car when it was impossible for the driver to avoid hitting it. The subjects reacted appropriately, but once told that the situation had been faked they were often very bitter toward the experimenter. Despite this and other evidence of great distress, the experiment continued until the planned number of subjects (18-20) had been tested. Later, another small study of a similar nature was conducted. Ultimately, about 30 subjects were exposed to this traumatic situation. (Ethical Principles in the Conduct of Research with Human Participants. American Psychological Association, Washington, D.C., 1973, page 74.)

4. In the process of developing textbooks, teaching materials, and standardized achievement tests in all subjects, researchers and experimenters often "try out" books on or administer tests to classes without first telling students of the experimental nature of the situation or asking them to volunteer. (Since the materials—particularly the tests—may not be of any real benefit to the students themselves, it might be questionable whether this sort of participation ought to be required of them.)

 © Winston Press, Inc. Permission is given to reproduce this page for student use.

RESEARCH WITH HUMAN PARTICIPANTS: II

1.   In order to learn more about the early stages of mental illness and to be able to focus on prevention as well as treatment, doctors would like to interveiw people who seem to have a tendency toward emotional instability or mental breakdown. To be told that they have been chosen for this type of study, however, would probably increase the subjects' likelihood of having mental disorders.

2.   In a study to discover the conditions under which people become curious about unusual events, a scene was staged in which actors started a loud argument in a city street. The subjects in the experiment were pedestrians who were interviewed <u>after</u> they had witnessed the incident <u>without</u> being told that it had been staged. The subjects were <u>never</u> told of their part in the experiment.

3.   In a study of the causes of prejudice, participants attended a series of lectures on anthropology which surreptitiously gave them false information designed to create negative attitudes toward people of a certain ethnic group. After being tested on their attitudes toward this minority group, subjects were told that they had been deceived.

4.   In a survey of drug use among students, it was necessary to identify students by name so that they could be located and questioned some two years later. Some of the students' answers were clearly self-incriminating. Although they promised to keep the names and answers confidential, the researchers wondered if the college or the courts could ever legally force them to disclose this information.

RESEARCH WITH HUMAN PARTICIPANTS: III

1.   Experimental testing of drugs is now commonly done at state penitentiaries with inmates as subjects. Many prisoners have little money, even for cigarettes or magazines. Researchers believe that if they pay prisoners the wages they would pay for outside volunteers, this would pressure many inmates into participating because it would take advantage of their financial need. They therefore keep the pay very low.

©Winston Press, Inc. Permission is given to reproduce this page for student use. 161

2. During a study of the effectiveness of vocational training for retarded young people, investigators questioned relatives, employers, and friends of the recent graduates of a state training program. They discovered that some employers and friends were not aware that the graduates had been given this training, or that they were legally designated as retarded.

3. In a study of methods of reducing hostility among people, members of two rival street gangs were recruited and underwent a fairly lengthy training session. The purpose of the experiment and the possibility that it would reduce the hostility between the members of these gangs were not revealed to the volunteers prior to the research because investigators felt that the participants would not want to volunteer if they knew why the training session was being conducted.

4. A researcher worked on the production line of a manufacturing plant. He was there as a participant-observer to collect data on human interactions which he recorded in detail for later analysis. The fact that he was a psychologist doing research was not known to his coworkers. Just as he was about to leave the job, however, he told the other workers that he was a psychologist and revealed to them the purpose of his working in the plant.

The Game Strategy

"Approval of Research": A Simulation

("Ethical Principles in Scientific Research with Human Participants" Continued)

A simple simulation strategy employing a few familiar research projects can be used to study the application of the APA guidelines in greater detail.

The class is divided into three groups: Researchers, Examiners, and Judges. The Researchers will be responsible for presenting a research proposal to the Examiners for their consideration of its potential effects on human participants. They will state the purpose of their research, the manner in which subjects will be recruited, and the procedures they

162 © Winston Press, Inc. Permission is given to reproduce this page for student use.

intend to carry out during the experiment. The simple Research
Proposal form which follows on page 166 will help this group to
organize its presentation. The Researchers' objective, of course,
is to get their proposal approved; they may agree to make
changes in the study only if they feel that the changes won't
affect the validity of their research.

The Examiners will be responsible for reviewing the
proposals in light of the ten APA ethical principles previously
presented. They will attempt to discover and question any
problems that may arise with the research, and they may
propose changes to protect the rights of human participants.
The Examiners should make as strong a case as possible
against the proposal, while the Researchers should argue
for it.

The third group, the Judges, will be responsible for
accepting or rejecting the proposal. They will listen to the
Researchers' presentation and the Examiners' criticisms, but
may not ask questions or make suggestions except for the
sake of clarification. The Researchers will obviously give as
favorable a presentation of their proposal as they can, while the
Examiners will be as critical as they can. The Judges will thus
be able to weigh or balance the considerations of both parties
without being committed in advance to the views of either one.

Each of these three roles approaches the situation from a
different perspective; students' feelings about these perspectives
may be discussed later. By rotating groups in these roles,
students will experience all of these perspectives and their
different sets of pressures and demands. Each of the three
groups, then, should be given the opportunity to play each role.

Organization
The presentation of this simulation is relatively simple.
Researchers will need time to prepare their presentations; it's
generally best if they propose research projects which have
already been studied in class so that they can use the course
textbooks as their resources. The teacher should choose and
assign the research proposals, however.

It's not necessary for the Researchers to present a study
exactly as it was carried out. They should, however, be
prepared to make a clear and coherent presentation as if

they're going to conduct the research themselves. They might, for example, have to invent a method of recruiting participants, especially if they don't know how this was done by the original investigators.

All three groups should prepare their research proposals simultaneously, since this aspect of the simulation takes time. (They will, of course, be working on different proposals.) A full class session may need to be devoted to this task, or it may be assigned as homework; students will not only have to organize their explanations, but will also have to attempt to foresee possible objections and questions. Communication skills of orderly presentation and explanation should be emphasized. The proposal form which follows may be expanded by means of many specific questions if the teacher feels that students will need more help in this regard.

Presentation and Examination
These two steps of the simulation are what comprise the interaction, so as much time as seems necessary should be allowed for them. All students should be provided with the Research Proposal forms (page 166) as well as with copies of the APA Principles (pages 159). During the follow-up discussion, the students can compare the three research proposals and offer their opinions concerning the place of behavioral research in society.

In everyday life, of course, more people end up as participants than researchers. (Incidentally, the U.S Census is one form of this type of research.) The benefits of this unit, however, aren't limited to future social scientists. By considering these situations from the three different perspectives outlined above, one can become quite conscious of his or her own rights as a possible participant. And in an age when the benefits and burdens of social scientific research are rapidly increasing, it's important that all people become more conscious of these rights and what they mean.

An Alternative Approach
Another possibility for this type of learning experience might involve the study of the use of animals (such as monkeys, rats, and so on) in research. What types of ethical principles should

apply here? Should they be different from the ones which apply to research which utilizes human subjects? What special considerations might be involved? (A recent collection of essays edited by Tom Regan and Peter Singer, Animals' Rights and Human Obligations, Englewood Cliffs, N.J.: Prentice Hall, 1975, might be of some help.)

The Concept Strategy

Identifying the Concept

"Kant's Practical Imperative": A Class Discussion

One of the best formulations of the value of integrity as a moral principle is that of the German philosopher Immanuel Kant:

> Act in such a way that you always treat humanity in your own person or in the person of any other, never simply as a means, but always at the same time as an end.

A brief explanation of Kant's principle might center on the following questions:

- What is an "end"?
- What is the distinction between "ends" and "means"?
- Does "never simply as a means" imply not as a means at all?
- What does "in your own person" imply?

With the class as a whole, or in small-group discussions, review the cases previously studied in the light of Kant's principle. Which decisions do treat people simply as means, and which don't? The objective of this discussion will primarily be that of identification, using Kant's principle as one formulation of the concept of integrity.

"Natural Rights": A Class Discussion

The value of integrity can also be viewed as a matter of respecting people's "natural rights." The concept of natural rights holds an important place not only in the history of moral thought but also in our political and legal traditions. A typical statement, and one which is good for stimulating class

RESEARCH PROPOSAL WORKSHEET

Research Title_____

Sponsor _____

1. What is the purpose of this research? What will it add to human knowledge? _____

_____

_____

2. Who will the participants be? How will they be recruited?____

_____

_____

3. What explanations of the research will be given to the participants? _____

_____

_____

4. What are the procedures of the experiment? _____

_____

_____

_____

5. Are there any follow-up procedures? _____

_____

_____

166 ©Winston Press, Inc. Permission is given to reproduce this page for student use.

discussion, is the following from the Declaration of Independence:

> We hold these truths to be self-evident: that all men are
> created equal, that they are endowed by their Creator
> with certain unalienable Rights, that among these are
> Life, Liberty, and the pursuit of Happiness.

Discussion might center on the following questions:

- What does "self-evident" mean? Would you agree that it's self-evident that people have these rights?
- Do the words "all men" apply to women as well? Why do you think the writers of the Declaration used the word "men"?
- What does "unalienable" mean? Does a person convicted of a crime give up his or her rights? If so, which ones? Which ones does he or she retain?
- What does "life" mean here? Is life an absolute right? What if the country forces individuals to risk their lives in war?
- Is the "pursuit of happiness" an absolute right? How must it be qualified or limited?
- Are there other natural rights? [Property, privacy, health, work.]

Explaining and Defining the Concept

The concept of integrity differs from the central value concepts of some of the other units in this Handbook in that it's given many names and is described in many ways—concern for others, consideration, caring, love (as used in religious formulations of religious principles), respect for others, and so on. One way to approach an explanation of the concept is to discuss the meanings of some of these related terms. The American Heritage Dictionary (New York, 1969) gives the following definitions (adapted and in part):

> Respect: 1. to feel or show esteem for, to honor;
> 2. to show some consideration for.
> Considerate: having regard for the needs and feelings of others.
> Love: (theology) the benevolence or kindness that people should rightly feel for one another.
> Concern: 1. to be of importance to; 2. regard for or interest in someone or something.
> Integrity: completeness, unity. Synonym: honor.
> Dignity: self-respect...that inspires respect.

Modeling the Concept

The outline of the Concept Strategy is found on pages 62-69; the facilitating questions are found on page 72. The following chart is just a starter.

Sample Concept Modeling Worksheet:

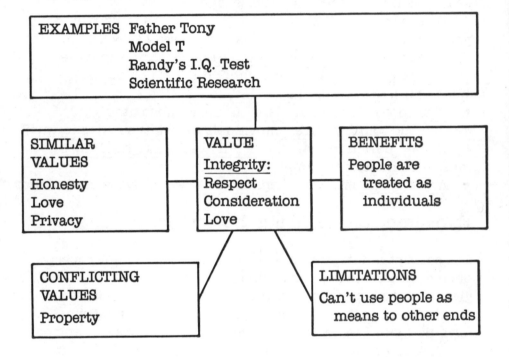

EXAMPLES   Father Tony
           Model T
           Randy's I.Q. Test
           Scientific Research

SIMILAR
VALUES

Honesty
Love
Privacy

VALUE
Integrity:
Respect
Consideration
Love

BENEFITS
People are
   treated as
   individuals

CONFLICTING
VALUES
Property

LIMITATIONS
Can't use people as
   means to other ends

Chapter 11:
Relationships:
A Marriage and Family or Personal Relations Unit

The Awareness Strategy

"Opinions on Family Life"

The awareness activities for this unit should not only direct students' attention to their own feelings about human relations, but should also help them to become aware of and appreciate the many different types of associations and family patterns that exist within our soceity.

The "Opinions on Family Life" worksheet is a good introduction to this unit. It can be used according to any of the teaching plans found in the section on the Awareness Strategy, pages 23-32.

"Ideal Families"

The title of this activity is intentionally misleading. The purpose of the exercise is to destroy the myth of the "ideal family" by illustrating the variety of ideal families people have in mind when they talk about family life.

The teacher asks students to write a paragraph or a single-page essay describing their own image of the ideal family. Some hints can be given about what the essay might include, but only if this seems absolutely necessary.

When the essays are completed, some students can be asked to read theirs aloud to the class. The teacher can put the following chart or table on the chalkboard and write notes in

The materials in this unit are presented sequentially, beginning with awareness activities which introduce the topic and ending with conceptual abstractions. They can be used in any order, however, according to the teacher's approach or the demands of the course in which they are included.

OPINIONS ON FAMILY LIFE WORKSHEET

Circle the word or phrase following each statement that comes closest to <u>your own</u> opinion.

1. Younger children get more privileges.

Always   Usually   Not Usually   Never

2. Children should have a say in family decisions.

Always   Sometimes   Not Much   Never

3. The father is and should be the natural authority in a family.

Agree   Don't Know   Disagree

4. Divorce is the best solution to some marriage problems.

Always   Sometimes   Not Very Often   Never

5. Parents should be able to tell their children whom to have as friends.

Always   Sometimes   Not Very Often   Never

6. Parents should never argue in front of their children.

Agree   Don't Know   Disagree

7. Grandparents should be encouraged to live with a family.

Agree   Don't Know   Disagree

8. Who should decide what to do on a vacation?

Father   Mother   Children   Whole Family

9. People who don't get married will never be happy.

Agree   Don't Know   Disagree

10. Both parents should hold jobs or have careers.

Never   Only if they have to   Only if they want to   Generally yes

170 © Winston Press, Inc. Permission is given to reproduce this page for student use.

IDEAL FAMILIES

Number of children

Place to live
[city, country, suburbs]

Authority
[father decides, mother has
some say, equal power]

Work
[one parent works, both work]

Raising children
[strict parents,
permissive parents, democratic]

©Winston Press, Inc. Permission is given to reproduce this page for student use.

the appropriate boxes characterizing each story after it is read. Students should be asked to help identify the items in each story; in some cases, the author of a story may have to add information that wasn't included in the original essay. Other characteristics should be added as students mention them.

"Important Qualities": Topics for Discussion

The following questions are meant to stimulate reflection and discussion. Students should answer them individually and then discuss their answers in small groups. They may change their answers if they wish, but don't have to (in fact, shouldn't) attempt to agree on a group list.
• What are the three most important characteristics of a good mother and wife?
• What are the three most important characteristics of a good father and husband?
• What are the three most important characteristics of a good sister or brother?
    Class discussion following the small-group discussions can be guided by the following questions:
• Did you change any of your answers during the discussion? Why or why not?
• Did the girls and boys [women and men] list different characteristics for good mothers and fathers? If so, why?

"The Generation Gap"

The following questionnaire is designed to help students become more aware of the differences among themselves and between themselves and their parents. Increased understanding and awareness of different feelings can build respect and lead to better relationships; the objective of the exercise, therefore, is to attempt to close the generation gap through understanding. The questionnaire has two steps; only after students have completed the first should they be given the directions for the second.
    Step I Directions to Students: The center of the questionnaire contains a number of simple questions. In

GENERATION GAP QUESTIONNAIRE

Column I	1. In your opinion, should the following be legal, or illegal?	Column II
Legal Illegal	A speech advocating Communism	Legal Illegal
Legal Illegal	A demonstration in a public park by the American Nazi Party	Legal Illegal
Legal Illegal	Wiretapping by the police	Legal Illegal

	2. Do you agree, or disagree?	
Agree Disagree	Most people who live in poverty could get jobs if they really wanted to.	Agree Disagree
Agree Disagree	The U.S. spends too much money on weapons.	Agree Disagree
Agree Disagree	Men are naturally more logical and scientific-minded than women.	Agree Disagree
Agree Disagree	The public schools generally do a good job.	Agree Disagree
Agree Disagree	Music is an important part of life.	Agree Disagree

©Winston Press, Inc. Permission is given to reproduce this page for student use. 173

Column I on the left, circle the answer that comes closest to your own opinion.

Step II Directions to Students: On the right side of the page, in Column II, circle the answer that you think your parents would give for each question. You can think of both parents together, or of just your mother or father. [The teacher may want to substitute the words "guardian" or "grandparent" or some other relative where applicable, both here and in the discussion questions which follow.]

Questions for Follow-up Discussion or Writing Assignments
• Are you generally like your parents in your views, or are you very different? Why?
• Which differences (if there are any) do you think are the most important? Why?
• Why do you think that you and your parents have different opinions on some issues?
• If your parents and grandparents were discussing these questions together, do you think that they'd agree, or disagree, with one another? Why?
• Do you think that your opinions will change as you get older? Why or why not? If so, how do you think they will change?

The Debate Strategy

Three Cases: "A New Job," "Summer Agreement," and "Not Allowed to Die"

The following cases can be used according to the outline of the Debate Strategy found on pages 33-42. Since Marriage and Family and Personal Relations courses often deal with issues which are within the realm of everyone's experience, this is one subject on which students can also be asked to write their own cases.

Other Debate Strategy cases in this Handbook which can be used in this unit include "Father Tony," page 148; "The Orphan," page 134; and "A Doctor's Choice," page 133.

A NEW JOB

Mr. and Mrs. Dayton were both schoolteachers. When they started having children, Mrs. Dayton quit her job and stayed home to raise the family.

In her spare time, however, she attended law school. She did so well that in five years she graduated and was offered a job with a law firm in Washington, D.C.

This posed a serious problem for the Daytons. If Mrs. Dayton took the job, the family would have to move to Washington. Mr. Dayton would have to give up his job, and there would be no guarantee that he'd be able to find another one.

The job would be an excellent opportunity for Mrs. Dayton, but they're both concerned about whether Mr. Dayton will be able to find a job.

Should the Daytons move, or shouldn't they?

SUMMER AGREEMENT

Jack and Jill have been going together for about a year. They're both high school juniors.

During this coming summer, Jill will be going to a sports camp for a month, and Jack will be going away for four weeks to a resort with his parents. They know that they'll miss seeing each other since they've spent a lot of time together, and both of them are wondering if they'll be making any other close friendships during the summer. The sports camp schedules lots of dances and social activities, and the resort usually plans plenty of movies and parties. Both Jack and Jill think it would be silly to refuse to participate in these activities, but neither of them has dated anyone else since they've started going together.

"I think you should go to the dances and socials," Jack says, "but just don't get too friendly with any boys."

"That's not fair," Jill answers. "Why should you tell me not to be friendly with anyone? I'll still want to go with you when I come back, and we'll be able to write to each other, but why shouldn't I be friends with any other boys? It would be okay with me if you went out with another girl. We can't limit our friendships just to each other. Why don't we just do what we want and agree not to ask each other any questions about it when we see each other in the fall?"

If you were Jack, would you agree?

©Winston Press, Inc. Permission is given to reproduce this page for student use. 175

NOT ALLOWED TO DIE

A letter published in a British medical journal told of a doctor who was admitted to a hospital with advanced stomach cancer. An operation revealed that his liver was also affected. Another operation followed, and there was evidence of further complications.

The patient was told of his condition and, since he was a doctor, he fully understood. Despite increasing doses of drugs, he suffered constant pain. Ten days after the second operation, he collapsed with a clot in a lung artery. This was removed by still another operation.

When he had sufficiently recovered, he expressed his appreciation of the good intentions and skills of the surgeon who had performed the last operation. Then he said, "If I have a further collapse, I don't want anything else to be done to prolong my life. The pain is more than I want to bear any longer."

The surgeon wrote a note to this effect on his case records, and the hospital staff knew of the patient's feelings.

A week later, the doctor suffered a heart attack. The surgeon told the doctor's wife that her husband would die if they didn't operate immediately. He said that he'd operate only if she gave him her permission.

If you were the doctor's wife, would you sign the permission form?

The Rational Strategy

Four Cases: "A Difficult Move," "Sarah," "Mrs. Crank," and "Rocky Tomatoes"

Family problems and decisions concerning personal friendships or community relations make ideal Rational Strategy cases because they're generally the kinds of issues where more than one alternative can be considered. The Rational Strategy is also especially useful here because students already have a great deal of experience to draw from when they're asked to imagine alternatives and predict consequences.

Once students become familiar with the procedures for the Rational Strategy, the outline worksheets for listing

 © Winston Press, Inc. Permission is given to reproduce this page for student use.

alternatives and consequences (pages 48 and 60) can usually be completed without much difficulty by students in small groups, using any of the following cases as handouts. Further explanation shouldn't be necessary.

Other Rational Strategy cases in this <u>Handbook</u> which can be used in this unit include "The Candy Store," page 119; "Randy's I.Q. Test," page 153; and "The Prom," page 135.

A DIFFICULT MOVE

Grandma Clark has been living alone for about ten years. Recently, though, her family has been getting worried about her ability to take care of herself.

About three weeks ago, she was hospitalized with a broken shoulder and is just now due to be released and go home again. Mr. and Mrs. Clark and their two children, Randy and Jane, have been visiting her regularly; they realize they'll have to work together to come up with a solution to the problem.

Grandma Clark is unable to lift things—her arm is still tied up—and won't be able to cook for herself for quite some time. She's been having difficulty walking for the last year or so, and this is a special problem, since the bathroom in her house is on the second floor. Her family is especially concerned that she may fall on the stairs and injure herself again.

In short, they've decided that Grandma can't be left to live by herself any longer. There seem to be three alternatives:

1.   She can move in with the Clarks, but this will mean that Randy, who's eleven years old, will have to give up his room and move in with Jane, who's six years old.

2.   She can move into a private retirement home, but this will mean that the Clarks will have to help her out financially. Her pension and social security benefits amount to $400 per month, which isn't enough. She would need at least $200 more per month, and if the Clarks decided to give this to her, they wouldn't be able to afford the new car they need or the improvements they want to make on their home. Eventually, this might even use up the money the Clarks have saved for Randy and Jane's college expenses.

3.   She can move to the county welfare retirement home. Although she says she's more than willing to go there, the

©Winston Press, Inc. Permission is given to reproduce this page for student use. 177

Clarks know that she wouldn't be happy and that she may even
feel that they don't want her.

What should they do? Are there any other alternatives
available to them? If so, what are they?

SARAH

Sarah's parents are very worried about her. She's
fourteen years old, does well in school, and is generally a
happy, pleasant girl. The problem is that Sarah doesn't seem to
like being a girl.

She hardly ever played with dolls or played "house"
when she was younger, and now she seems mostly interested in
boys' sports and games. She refuses to wear dresses and has
only one girlfriend, Kate; unfortunately, she hasn't seen Kate
very often since Kate's family moved to the next town. Sarah
plays mostly with her brothers, Jeff and Bill, who are both
older than she is, or with two other boys who live in the
neighborhood. One is her age, and the other is a year younger.
Sarah says that she doesn't want to get married or have
children; she likes mechanical things (including motorcycles)
and thinks that she might become an engineer or a mechanic
when she grows up.

When Sarah was younger, her parents thought that she
was just a tomboy and would grow out of it. She hasn't,
though. Now she says that she isn't interested in going to any
of the social events at school.

What should Sarah's parents do?

MRS. CRANK

Jack and Sandy Marcus live next to Mrs. Crank. Mrs.
Crank frequently yells at them for walking on her lawn or
complains to their parents when she thinks they're making too
much noise. Once she even called Mrs. Marcus on the telephone
because Jack and Sandy were roller skating in front of her
house. And when Jack's dog wandered into her yard, she
threatened to call the police.

One day when Jack and Sandy were playing kickball, the
ball went over the fence and through the glass window of a
small outdoor planter that Mrs. Crank grew flowers in. Luckily,
Mrs. Crank wasn't home, so Jack ran into her yard and got the
ball back.

 ©Winston Press, Inc. Permission is given to reproduce this page for student use.

They told their mother what had happened but said that they were afraid to tell Mrs. Crank about it. They thought that she'd even be angry because Jack had gone into her yard to retrieve the ball.

If you were Mrs. Marcus, what would you do?

ROCKY TOMATOES

Vincent Koval and two of his friends decided to go out trick-or-treating together on Halloween night. As they were passing the school, they noticed that Mr. Henry's garden was full of ripe tomatoes.

"Look at all those tomatoes!" Mike said. "Wouldn't it be fun to leave a crushed one on someone's doorstep if the person who lives there won't give us a treat?"

"I think it would be an even better idea to splatter a couple on Mr. Pyle's classroom window," Dick answered. "He's such a grouch, he deserves it."

Without another thought, the three boys started gathering tomatoes and tossing them toward Mr. Pyle's room at the corner of the building. After three or four tomatoes had reached their target, Mike picked up a rock and threw it. There was a sound of breaking glass. At that point, Mr. Henry came out of his house, and the boys ran away.

The next morning, the three boys were called into the office of the school principal, Mr. Cook.

"Mr. Henry has told me that you boys were in his garden last night," he said sternly. "I want to know who broke the window in Mr. Pyle's room."

The boys looked at one another, and all denied having thrown the rock. They admitted that they'd been out together and that they'd thrown tomatoes at the window, but they refused to say which one of them had actually broken the window.

"In that case," Mr. Cook answered, "I'll have to punish all of you equally. Until one of you tells me who broke the window, none of you will be allowed to participate in any school activities. This means no sports, parties, or clubs. There's been too much vandalism around here, and we have to put a stop to it!"

©Winston Press, Inc. Permission is given to reproduce this page for student use.

Mr. Cook also called the parents of each of the boys. When Vince's parents confronted him, he told them that Mike had broken the window. "I don't want to tell on my friend, though," he said. "I'm afraid that Mike would get in a lot of trouble and that he wouldn't like me any more."

If you were Vince's parents, what would you do?

The Game Strategy

"Partner Choice": A Marriage Decisions Game

The purpose of this game is to give students experience in becoming aware of and judging the many factors that may be involved in choosing a mate. The game can take anywhere from two to four class periods, depending on individual class needs, the number of students, and the instructor's particular teaching style.

Discussion is important for this game to be truly effective, of course, but it's best to limit it somewhat during the game itself. Otherwise, students may get the feeling that the teacher expects certain responses or that there's a "right" or "wrong" way to play.

Strategy and Interaction

At the beginning of the first session, the teacher should briefly explain the purpose of the game. Generally, it's sufficient to say that this game will familiarize the students with the kinds of choices people are faced with when they're thinking about getting married. Too much explanation can be self-defeating; it's best to let students get the point of the game by playing it.

A very limited discussion of which areas of life might be considered most important and which least important can follow. This can go on just long enough to help students realize that there are real differences in degree of importance, but not long enough to allow any class agreement to emerge on specific points.

This game was developed with the assistance of Mr. George Burns and some of his students at Brooke County High School in West Virginia.

The teacher then distributes the Step I Values Worksheet (page 182). This may or may not require an oral explanation, depending on the class. Students should be given sufficient time to complete their worksheets. (This should be an individual effort, not a group project.) The teacher should emphasize that students must state their own opinions on the worksheets.

It may be necessary to draw the students through the worksheet step by step. For each question, the teacher may ask, "Why is this an important area?" and "What could happen if partners didn't agree on this?" Discussion of which area is most important should be avoided, however.

After the Values Worksheet has been completed, the teacher distributes the Step II Interests, Desires, and Expectations Worksheet (page 184). Depending on time limits, this can take place either at the end of the first session or the beginning of the second. Again, the worksheet is self-explanatory; the teacher may want to emphasize that students should concentrate on their own opinions. Since it's a fairly straightforward exercise, no discussion should be necessary before or after.

After completing their worksheets, the students choose partners from among their classmates. Since this choice can be a complicated and anxiety-causing process, the teacher may want to make up his or her own procedures rather than utilizing any standard one. The following suggestions may prove helpful.

Basically, students are asked to compare their Step II opinions worksheets with those of other students for the purpose of finding a partner whose interests, desires, and expectations agree with their own. This process can be left entirely open; the teacher may simply encourage the students to walk around the classroom and compare their worksheets with others' until they've each found a satisfactory partner. If this is done, however, it might be best if students are asked to compare their worksheets with everyone else's; if there isn't enough emphasis on this comparison, they may just choose the people sitting next to them. Students will probably be more worried about finding a partner than they will be about finding a good or compatible one; they won't want to be left alone at the end of the selection process. Thus, it's important to allow enough time for the comparisons to take place.

PARTNER CHOICE:
STEP I VALUES WORKSHEET

Name: _____

People who are planning to get married are faced with a number of decisions and choices. Listed below are nine aspects of life which are generally considered to be very important. You are to number them in order of their importance (value) to <u>you</u>, beginning with what <u>you</u> think is <u>most</u> important and ending with what <u>you</u> think is <u>least</u> important.

_____ 1.   HOME. (Would you rather live in a city, or in the country? Do you prefer an apartment, or a house? How important do you think a specific type of home environment is to a couple's happiness?)

_____ 2.   RELIGION. (How important is religion to you? What if you were Jewish, for example, and the person you wanted to marry was Catholic? Do you think that religious differences can cause great problems between people, or are they relatively unimportant in light of other factors?)

_____ 3.   POLITICS. (Liberals and conservatives can disagree a lot. What if you were a Democrat, for example, and the person you wanted to marry was a Republican? What if you were a Socialist and the person you wanted to marry didn't care at all about politics?)

_____ 4.   INCOME. (Everybody would like to have a lot of money, but that isn't always possible. What if both you and the person you wanted to marry had low-paying jobs? Would that make a difference?)

_____ 5.   EDUCATION. (How important is it that you and your prospective partner have similar educational backgrounds? What if you were a lawyer, for example, and the person you wanted to marry hadn't even finished high school? Would this make a difference to your future together?)

_____ 6.   AUTOMOBILES. (What you might like and what you're able to afford might be two different things. And what if the person you wanted to marry didn't know how to drive?)

182 ©Winston Press, Inc. Permission is given to reproduce this page for student use.

_____ 7. CHILDREN. (How important is it that you and your prospective partner agree on the number of children—if any—you want to have? What kind of parent would you be—strict, or permissive? How important is it to determine these things before getting married?)

_____ 8. LIFESTYLE. (There are many day-to-day living arrangements that need to be made once two people start sharing a household. Who will do the housework, for example? Who will pay the bills?)

_____ 9. LEISURE. (How many interests should two people who are planning to get married have in common? What if the man likes to go hunting, for example, and the woman doesn't? What if the woman is an avid bridge player and the man isn't? What about separate vacations?)

Now fill in the chart below according to how you ranked the items above.

MOST IMPORTANT

(1) _____ 5 Value Points

(2) _____ 5 Value Points

(3) _____ 4 Value Points

(4) _____ 4 Value Points

(5) _____ 3 Value Points

(6) _____ 3 Value Points

(7) _____ 2 Value Points

(8) _____ 2 Value Points

LEAST IMPORTANT

(9) _____ 1 Value Point

PARTNER CHOICE:
STEP II INTERESTS, DESIRES, AND EXPECTATIONS WORKSHEET

Name: _____

In the space after each letter, write the number of the answer which <u>best</u> shows <u>your own</u> interest, desire, or expectation.

A. _____ HOME: Where will you expect to live?
    (1) City apartment
    (2) Suburban house
    (3) Country house
    (4) Farm
    (5) Mobile home

B. _____ RELIGION: Which of the following describes your religious preference?
    (1) Protestant
    (2) Jewish
    (3) Catholic
    (4) Other
    (5) None

C. _____ POLITICS: Which of the following describes your political leanings?
    (1) Liberal
    (2) Moderate liberal
    (3) Moderate conservative
    (4) Conservative
    (5) Not interested in politics

D. _____ INCOME: What salary level do you expect to achieve?
    (1) Below $10,000 (Store clerk, part-time employment)
    (2) $10,000-$15,000 (Government or factory worker, teacher)
    (3) $15,000-$20,000 (Skilled worker, carpenter, plumber)
    (4) $20,000-$25,000 (Scientific technician, banker, business person)
    (5) Over $25,000 (Doctor, lawyer)

E. _____ EDUCATION: Which of the following describes <u>your</u> plans at the present time?
    (1) Won't finish high school.
    (2) Will graduate from high school.

 ©Winston Press, Inc. Permission is given to reproduce this page for student use.

(3) Will attend technical or junior college (two years).

(4) Will be a college graduate (four years).

(5) Will achieve advanced degrees
(required for doctors or lawyers,
for example).

F. _____ AUTOMOBILES: What do you <u>expect</u> to be able to
afford?

(1) VW or Toyota

(2) Ford or Chevrolet

(3) Pickup truck or camper

(4) Cadillac or Lincoln Continental

(5) Mercedes or foreign sports car

G. _____ CHILDREN: Which of the following would <u>you</u>
prefer, and which type of parents would you
like you and your partner to be?

(1) No children

(2) Small family (two or fewer children),
strict parents

(3) Small family (two or less children),
permissive parents

(4) Large family (more than two
children), strict parents

(5) Large family (more than two children),
permissive parents

H. _____ LIFESTYLE: Which of the following do you agree
with <u>most</u>?

(1) Housework should always be shared equally.

(2) The husband should do some of the housework.

(3) The husband should help as an
occasional favor.

(4) A man should help only if his wife works.

(5) It's all woman's work.

I. _____ LEISURE: Which do you like <u>most</u>?

(1) Wilderness activities (hunting, camping)

(2) Outdoor sports (skiing, tennis, baseball)

(3) Indoor sports (bowling, billiards)

(4) Indoor social events (parties, T.V. with friends)

(5) Being alone (hobbies, T.V., reading)

©Winston Press, Inc. Permission is given to reproduce this page for student use.

The teacher may instead choose to assign students to small groups (from four to five students each). This will allow them to discuss their similarities and differences freely. The groups should be changed once or twice before students are allowed to make their choices. This will encourage them to take their time, and they'll be less apt to just team up with friends or the first people they meet. It can slow down the eager students and draw out the quieter ones.

Or the teacher may wish to begin the selection process with a class discussion during which a few students are asked to describe the areas they value most and the choices they made on their worksheets. This will demonstrate that real differences exist; when similarities appear, the teacher can suggest that students compare other interest choices. When the idea of serious comparison has been established, open class interaction can be attempted.

However the teacher decides to implement this step, students should be given sufficient time to carry it out to their satisfaction. They might even be encouraged to change choices if, after further discussion and comparison, they think a better one might be possible. Some students may get more than one partnership offer and have to decide among them.

Some assistance from the teacher might be needed at the end of this interaction phase. A few remaining students can be "assigned" to each other, but it should be made very clear that these choices are forced and that allowances will be made because of this. (Discussion of what happens when people are forced into marriage may be appropriate later.) If there are more students of one sex than the other, as there probably will be, students may have to form partnerships with others of the same sex. To avoid embarrassment or silliness, the teacher may explain at the outset that unequal numbers will necessitate partnerships of two boys or two girls in order to play the game through.

The game can also be played with three-person partnerships. If, for example, there are twice as many students of one sex, this may work very well. One of the three will have to fill in two Step III worksheets, but this shouldn't take too much time. (The game can be played in single-sex classes as well as coeducational ones, if the teacher is careful to preface it with a brief explanation.)

After all students have chosen or been assigned to partners, the Step III Partner Comparison Worksheets (page 188) are distributed. Again, students should be given enough time to fill them out to their satisfaction.

Following the students' completion of their worksheets, the teacher should conduct a discussion on the results. It's best if the discussion goes backward, beginning with questions about the scores and then exploring the reasons for the scores. The following discussion questions might prove helpful:

• How did your score come out?
• What was your partner's score?
• Do you think that the score shows how good a partner choice you made? Why or why not?
• How could you or your partner get a higher (lower) score? What makes scores high or low?
• Is this game really a competitive one? [The teacher should lead students to realize that it isn't.]

The teacher may want to encourage students to raise objections to the game itself, if they wish. For example, he or she might ask the students,

• Is this a good game or a poor game? Why?
• Are there other areas or considerations that should have been included in the game but weren't? [These might include nationality, sexual compatibility, popularity, friends, e.g.]

The more students tear the game apart, the more aspects of partner decision-making they're apt to realize.

The fourth step is an even more "contrived" choice simulation; hence, perceptive students may raise further objections to the game later.

The teacher distributes the Step IV Compromise Worksheets (page 189) and allows students enough time to complete them. The following questions may be used for discussion and/or writing assignments:

• Who did most of the compromising? In which areas?
• Is agreement sometimes not necessary in order for people to get along with each other?
• Which partner had the highest score? Why do you think this happened?
• If you could, would you go back to the Step II worksheet and change any of the choices you made there? Why or why not? (Questions continue on page 190.)

PARTNER CHOICE:
STEP III PARTNER COMPARISON WORKSHEET

Name: _____

Listed below are the nine values or interests you compared with your partner. In the second column, check only those on which you agree. You may refer to your Step II worksheets if necessary.

In the third column, list the Value Points for each of the areas. (This will be a combined total—your points and your partner's points taken together.) You are to list only the points for the agreement areas you've checked—that is, those on which you and your partner agree. You may refer to your Step I worksheets if necessary.

VALUE AREA	PARTNER AGREEMENT (Compare your Step II worksheet with your partner's.)	VALUE POINTS (Consult your own Step I worksheet and your partner's; write combined points here.)
A. HOME	_____	_____
B. RELIGION	_____	_____
C. POLITICS	_____	_____
D. INCOME	_____	_____
E. EDUCATION	_____	_____
F. AUTOMOBILES	_____	_____
G. CHILDREN	_____	_____
H. LIFESTYLE	_____	_____
I. LEISURE	_____	_____

 © Winston Press, Inc. Permission is given to reproduce this page for student use.

PARTNER CHOICE:
STEP IV COMPROMISE WORKSHEET

Name: _____

1. There are probably many areas in which you and your partner do not agree. Look again at your Step II worksheets. Then list in the left-hand column below all of those areas in which you and your partner have different opinions. Make sure to list the choices each of you made.

DID NOT AGREE   COMPROMISE CHOICE

_____   _____

_____   _____

_____   _____

_____   _____

_____   _____

2. Now try to come to a compromise with your partner in each of the areas listed above. You may end up agreeing on your original choice, your partner's original choice, or an entirely new choice that you'll both be happy with. Write the choice in the right-hand column under Number 1 above.

3. If any of the compromise decisions are the same as your original choice, add your value points for that item to your total score. If any are the same as your partner's original choice, he or she should add the value points to his or her score. If you agreed on a new choice, both you and your partner can add half of the value points to your scores.

Enter Compromise Points Here: _____

                                                 _____

                                                 _____

Previous Score (from Step III Worksheet):   _____

                                        TOTAL: _____

4. Add your new score and   Your Score: _____
your partner's new score:
                              Partner's Score: _____

                    Partnership Score (TOTAL):   _____

©Winston Press, Inc. Permission is given to reproduce this page for student use. 189

- Would you change your priorities list if you could?
- What do you think the final personal and partnership scores mean?
- Do you think that this game is like real life? Why or why not?
- What if, in real life, people had to fill out long questionnaires before they were allowed to get married? [This question could briefly touch on computer dating services.]

"Sharing": A Communal Living Simulation

Communal living is a lifestyle which requires participants to share goods, property, and responsibility. Although the term was used a lot during the 1960's and early 1970's, and many people seem to believe that the concept originated during those years, people have been living in communes throughout history. Jesus' disciples provide one example; other communal groups include monastic orders from the Middle Ages down to the present; religious and economic communities which flourished in nineteenth-century America; homesteading communities and colonies in all ages; contemporary Utopian experiments; and modern urban living arrangements. The purpose of this simulation is to demonstrate some of the economic and human relations aspects of communal living and decision-making.

Before beginning the simulation, it may be helpful if the teacher provides the students with some background. Otherwise they may immediately equate communes with the contemporary "hippie" communes which have been so widely publicized. For every individual living in such a commune in the United States, there are probably twenty more living in religious or monastic communities. And if we count college and university dormitory life, which can certainly be considered communal living arrangements, the ratio would be even larger. Nor should we ignore the communal living circumstances of the military service. Background information on communes can be found in almost any encyclopedia under Monasticism, Utopia,

This simulation was developed by George Burns, Janet Rodriguez, and Robert T. Hall with the help of students at Brooke County High School and Wheeling Park High School in West Virginia.

Franciscans, Dominicans, Shakers, Amana, Oneida, and many other headings.

In addition to providing this background to enable students to get a "total" impression of the subject, it also might be a good idea to have a guest speaker come to class either before or after the simulation. A member of a local monastery or convent would probably be happy to contribute.

During the simulation, students are first asked to state some of their personal preferences concerning lifestyles; these statements are put aside for later reference. Students then organize into communal units in which they must decide on living arrangements, jobs and incomes, and communal and personal expenditures. After both communal and individual decisions have been made, the two types are evaluated and compared.

This simulation has provided a realistic experience for many students. Some have decided that they would seriously consider living communally, while others (some of whom were more favorably disposed to communal living at the outset) have decided that they wouldn't be very happy with such an arrangement. Almost all seemed more realistic in their evaluations at the end of the simulation, however.

This simulation calls upon the teacher to get very involved in arranging details, especially in his or her role as "employment officer." The teacher should take a free hand with this. In one class, for example, a student wanted a job as a preacher. The teacher simply told him that he could earn whatever money any other students in any of the communes put down on their personal expenses as "church contributions."

The Game Plan

Step I: Personal Preference Worksheets (page 196). These should be filled out individually. The purpose of this step is to get some indication of students' likes and dislikes and to attach value points to them. These will be used to judge their later decisions. On the left side of the sheet are thirty activities; students should be instructed to arrange these on the spaces at the right, putting those they like most at the top and those they dislike most at the bottom.

Step II: Organizing Communes.　The Communal Living Simulation is constructed for communes of about eight people. If it's used with smaller or larger groups, adjustments in the expenses for food, housing, utilities, and fuel will be necessary.

Students may be divided into communes by any method —friends may group together, or membership may be assigned. Commune members may all be of the same sex, or they may be mixed.

When the communes have been established, members should first decide how they're going to make future decisions. Some possible alternatives may be listed on the chalkboard; these could include the following:

- Majority vote
- Unanimous vote (everyone must agree)
- One leader (who makes all final decisions)
- A committee of three

Only when students have arranged some form of organization for decision-making should they go on to Step III.

Step III: Communal Decisions.　This step will require two or three class periods.

The "Community Expenses" (page 198), "Community Income" (page 200), and "Personal Spending Money" (page 201) worksheets should be distributed, along with the "House Job" cards (page 204), as follows:

1. Community Expenses—1 worksheet per commune.

2. Community Income—1 worksheet per commune.

3. Personal Spending Money—1 worksheet per person.

4. House Jobs—Each commune should receive 21 cooking, 21 kitchen cleanup, 14 housework, 4 repairs, 4 laundry, and 4 shopping cards. (The teacher should make 7 copies of the House Jobs sheet for each commune and discard 3 Laundry, 3 Shopping, and 3 Repair cards.)

It doesn't matter in what order the students make their decision—they'll figure it out.

Each commune will need to make the following arrangements; these may be written on the chalkboard or announced:

- Decide who works and who doesn't. (All may work, or some may do more house jobs. Use the Community Income worksheets.)

- Calculate expenses. (Use the Community Expense worksheets.)
- Distribute House Job cards in whatever way you decide. No one can hold more than 25 house jobs; members may trade jobs if they wish, or pay others to do them out of their spending money. (Add the same amount to the other person's spending money as is deducted from the spending money of the person who's paying.)
- Distribute personal spending money. (Deduct from Community Expenses the amounts added to Personal Spending Money worksheets.)

Employment.   It seems to work best if the teacher runs an "employment office," giving out jobs to people who apply for them. The teacher should interview applicants, asking them about their skills and experience (the teacher should presume that all participants are just graduating from high school; i.e., they have no special skills or professions). The teacher will want to give some students better jobs and some students worse ones—while some may be allowed to have the jobs they want, others might have to take whatever they get. The pay offered should be kept roughly to the following scale:

1. Salesperson, Waitress, Clerk, or anything comparable:

$3 per hour × 40 hours = $120 per week
Less deductions   15
Take-home pay $105 per week

2. Manual Labor (factory, construction) or anything comparable:

$4 per hour × 40 hours = $160
Less deductions   25
Take-home pay $135 per week

3. Creative work (crafts done at home):
$35 per week take-home pay

4. Part-time job:
$40 per week take-home pay

5. Unemployment
$30 per week take-home pay

All expenses and income are to be calculated on a weekly basis.

Step IV: Personal Evaluations.   After communal decisions have been made, each student should fill out a

Personal Evaluation Worksheet (page 202). The score on this sheet is intended to indicate how well a student's activities agree with the preferences he or she originally stated. Students should be instructed to place points in the plus or minus column only for those activities or things which they or their community have chosen to do. Employment points come from the preference sheet for whichever job(s) the students actually had.

Note that the employment points (whether plus or minus) are multiplied by 5 and that household jobs are figured according to the number of cards the person holds, multiplied by his or her own preference points for each job. (It sometimes helps to let students redistribute their household jobs while they're doing the evaluations.)

Step V: Discussion.   The following questions may be used to draw attention to the various aspects of the simulation:
• What does the final score show? [How well decisions coordinate with preferences.]
• How could your commune have been better organized?
• How did you change your living arrangements and activities after trying to balance your budget?
• Which people in your group would be happiest living in a commune? Why? Which people would be least happy? Why?
• How do the scores of commune members compare? Why are some higher or lower than others?
• Do you think that you would be happy in a commune like the one you've formed?

Step VI: Communal Problems—A Replay Adding a Community Crisis.   Once the communes have completed their evaluations, they may be given one of the following problems to face. These may be initiated by asking some of the commune members to role play the parts of the key people in each problem situation, or they may simply be announced:
• Two people want to get married and have a child. The two may be chosen from within the commune; or, if the original communes contained all boys or all girls, two students may be selected from each and one couple can be sent back to each commune.

This will require $500 for hospital and doctor expenses and will add 14 Child Care House Job cards to the commune. (There are no rules as to whether the couple has to get permission from their commune to get married or not; that is for them to decide.)

- (a) One person (either a volunteer or the person with the lowest score) wants to leave the commune. Reorganization is necessary to correct the budget and redistribute house jobs.

   (b) Two people (those who quit other communes) want to join.

- One person wants to go to college, which will cost $75 per week and will cut his or her income in half (if he or she has any) and limit him or her to 5 house jobs.

After working on their problems, students should report on whatever reorganization the communes made in an attempt to solve them.

   Follow-Up. A writing assignment is nearly always appropriate for closing this simulation. Topics could include:

- How our commune could have been better organized.
- Financial vs. personal problems—which are more important?
- Why I would/would not want to live in a commune.

The Concept Strategy

Three concepts emerge naturally out of the activities of this unit: friendship, family, and community. All three are closely related, of course, but it may be helpful to separate them for concept analysis and development.

   The friendship concept (which includes marriage) focuses on the relationships which exist between two people; the family concept emphasizes children; and the community concept highlights the wider circle of possible social arrangements.

   The Concept Strategy outline is described on pages 62-69; the Facilitating Questions are found on page 72. The diagrams which follow are only starters.

SHARING: PERSONAL PREFERENCES WORKSHEET

Name: _____

1.	Shopping for groceries	_____	+5
2.	Cooking	_____	+5
3.	Kitchen cleanup	_____	+5
4.	Job: salesperson, waiter or waitress, clerk	_____	+5
5.	Job: manual labor (factory)	_____	+5
6.	Creative job (music, pottery, crafts)	_____	+3
7.	Having a dog or cat	_____	+3
8.	Watching T.V.	_____	+3
9.	Reading (books, magazines)	_____	+3
10.	Housework (cleaning)	_____	+3
11.	Repairs (carpentry, painting)	_____	+1
12.	Doing the laundry	_____	+1
13.	Good food	_____	+1
14.	Cheap meals	_____	+1
15.	Stereo music	_____	+1

196 ©Winston Press, Inc. Permission is given to reproduce this page for student use.

16.	Luxury car	_____	−1
17.	Economy car	_____	−1
18.	Going to parties	_____	−1
19.	Movies	_____	−1
20.	Fashionable clothes	_____	−1
21.	Plain clothes	_____	−3
22.	Going out for pizza	_____	−3
23.	Sports (bowling, golf)	_____	−3
24.	Living with a roommate	_____	−3
25.	Having a private room	_____	−3
26.	Vacationing at home	_____	−5
27.	Vacationing away from home	_____	−5
28.	Musical instrument	_____	−5
29.	_____	_____	−5
30.	_____	_____	−5

©Winston Press, Inc. Permission is given to reproduce this page for student use. 197

SHARING: COMMUNITY EXPENSES WORKSHEET

House (urban or suburban area)

1. Rent   Old House   New House $_____
   4 bedrooms $65/week $100/week
   8 bedrooms $100/week $125/week

2. Repairs and household expenses $_____
   Old house: $25/week
   New house: $10/week

3. Automobile
   Economy car: $30/week $_____
   Luxury car: $50/week $_____
   Gas and oil: $25/week (each car) $_____
   Automobile insurance: $5/week (each car) $_____
   (Only four members may claim the use
   of one car for enjoyment. If more wish
   to claim this, a second car will be
   necessary.)

4. Food $_____
   Choose one: Cheap meals: $100/week
                 Good food: $130/week

5. Utilities $_____
   Telephone, water, electricity: $30/week

6. Appliance payments $_____
   $15/week

7. Heat $_____
   Fuel: $20/week

8. Stereo (optional) $_____
   $5/week

9. Laundry $_____
   $6/week

10. T.V. (optional) $_____
    $5/week

11. Spending money $_____
    $_____ per person
    Multiplied by number of persons:

TOTAL WEEKLY EXPENSES: $_____

198 © Winston Press, Inc. Permission is given to reproduce this page for student use.